THE
BEGINNING ANTIQUE COLLECTOR'S
HANDBOOK

THE

Beginning Antique Collector's

HANDBOOK

AND GUIDE TO 1,000 ITEMS TO COLLECT

by

ANN KILBORN COLE

DAVID McKAY COMPANY, INC.
NEW YORK

ACKNOWLEDGMENTS

I WOULD like to thank the staffs of *Antiques, Hobbies,* the *Antique Journal,* and *Spinning Wheel* for their help in tracing collections and associations for me. Also the many dealers without whose help I would have been much longer in getting the facts of this book together. Too, I want to thank the Philadelphia *Inquirer* for the use of pictures used with my articles over the last six years and the individual collectors whose cooperation made this book possible. The cooperation of the museums has been most gratifying, especially that of the Metropolitan Museum in New York, the Museum of the Chester County Historical Society in West Chester, Pennsylvania; the recently established John Nelson Bergstrom Museum of Neenah, Wisconsin; the Essex Institute of Salem, Massachusetts; the Mary Earle Gould Museum of Worcester, Massachusetts; Norcross Greeting Cards, New York City; Stony Point Gallery of Stony Point, New York; Shaker Museum of Chatham, New York; Corning Glass Center, Corning, New York; Museum of the Home Insurance Company, New York City; Philadelphia Museum of Art, the Free Library of Philadelphia; Pennsylvania Farm Museum, Landisville, Pennsylvania; Washington Historical Museum of Valley Forge, Pennsylvania; the Wedgwood Museum of Merion, Pennsylvania; the Bucks County Historical Society, Mercer Museum of Doylestown, Pennsylvania; Shelburne Museum, Shelburne, Vermont; and the various commercial firms who allowed me access to their collections.

CONTENTS

ILLUSTRATIONS

following page 82

INTRODUCTION

COLLECTING is an instinct born into many of us, a bent acquired by others. Some give it free rein all their lives from the cradle to the grave. Others dab at it. Some give it only wishful thinking or do it vicariously through the confirmed collectors they may know. A few, but only a few, never give it a thought. There have always been collectors, and our museums testify to the expenditure of the time, efforts, and money of those earlier ones who went after the best—and got it. It was then the hobby of savants, of moneyed and leisured generations many of whom believed rightly that it was not only a pleasure and time passer but a duty to preserve the arts and crafts of early America from oblivion. We owe much to these early collectors.

But curiously, as taxes increased, money and time grew tighter and the supply of fine collectibles dwindled, collecting became more popular and widespread, moving down the social and economic scale to people like you and me, until today there has come into being a whole new generation of what are called *beginning collectors*. This is owing to the tremendous popular interest in antiques generally, the greater familiarity with them through the growth of shops outside the big cities; the shows, even the small local ones as well as the large publicized ones; museums, old ones with new wings for antiques and many new small ones; an avalanche of books, magazines for the amateur as well as the informed collector;

nation-wide organizations devoted to antiques and collecting; and last the prevalence of do-it-yourself helps such as sanders, lamp converters, polishes, cements, reproduction brasses, frames, wire display racks, and so on. Eventually almost everyone lands on the antiques bandwagon and also eventually most of the riders become collectors in a narrower sense.

The search for antique treasure is becoming increasingly hard because of the numbers of collectors which brings about a consequent scarcity of fine things and resulting higher prices. Hence collecting fields are opening up which might have been scoffed at even twenty years ago. Imagine Henry Dupont, George Horace Lorimer, or George McKearin with their pewter and luster and Stiegel glass taking seriously such things as ring trees or calendar plates. Yet there is just as much fun and justification in these humbler collections of today.

The term *beginning collectors* as opposed to *advanced collectors* is a recognized one in the field of antiques today. These are the amateurs whose interest in antiques is recent but who may not stay amateurs long when their time and zeal and money spur them on. These beginners may have learned a few things on the way as they picked up old pieces in the way of furniture for their homes; glass and silver for their old tables; china for their corner cupboards; iron and brass for their fireplaces, and so on. But their interest is still fairly diffused. We may call them antique collectors but not collectors in a specialized sense. Their field is the widest of all, and until they narrow down they are not *beginning collectors* as the term is used right now.

Many books have been written devoted to one phase of antiques, like American silver or art glass or mechanical banks. They have done much to promote interest and widen knowledge along specialized lines. Still other books cover specific and well-known collectibles chapter by chapter. All are good reading for the beginning collector when he has become inducted into the fold. But little has been written for the uninformed or meagerly informed lover of antiques who wants to narrow down his interest to one thing, to start collecting, and who does not know what to collect or how to go about it.

It would seem that collecting should not have to be taught or guided, that it is as simple an accomplishment as learning to ride a bicycle—nothing to it. You get on and you ride, wobbling until you get your balance. In other words, you just go out and buy the thing that interests you most until you have enough on your shelves or in your cupboard to brag about. But any confirmed collector will tell you that there is much more to it than that. There are "tricks of the trade" here as in any profession or hobby. There are limitations, pitfalls, hazards, all kinds of things to discourage the beginning collector until he falls by the wayside, a casualty of ignorance. Many small collections are standing forgotten and neglected because the beginner did not know what to expect when he started buying apostle spoons or Parian pitchers.

It is for such collectors that this book is written. It has been assembled in the same way and aimed at the same public as my first book on antiques. It is another starter book, packed with information both significant and trivial and recognizing the problems of the amateur collector as I have met them in the years when I have been writing for, meeting, and corresponding with those who do not know too much about antiques but who want to. In telling this story of beginning collecting I have called upon Rudyard Kipling's "six honest serving men," whose names are "What and Why and When xivINTRODUCTION

and How and Where and Who" because I feel the answers to these questions cover the whole field.

The book is concerned only with what are generally called antiques and eliminates such highly specialized fields of col- lecting as stamps, books, coins, currency, autographs, medals, records, prints, guns, old cars, Indian artifacts, primitive art of other lands, shells, rocks, and similar items. Perhaps occasionally the lists of articles suggested in this book will overlap with the above-mentioned categories but it will be only because the classification of "antique" justifies it. Collecting, which includes the new as well as the old, is not, strictly speaking, the concern of the collector whom I am addressing in this book except for the conscious collecting of current or not too old pieces which can be called the antiques of tomorrow and are cannily cornered today with an eye on their worth a generation from now. Or sometimes you might want to include new pieces in the collections of children or young people to stimulate their interest in collecting.

Please bear with me if at times I descend to the basic ABC's of collecting which may seem obvious to many of you. I promise to open up other aspects that may not be so familiar, in fact some that may never have occurred to the beginning collector who is on the way as being important enough to investigate. I hope it will lead every reader to happier and more intelligent collecting until he matriculates into the more rarefied areas of the advanced collectors. Then he may be able to tell *me* something!

A.K.C.

THE
BEGINNING ANTIQUE COLLECTOR'S
HANDBOOK

1.

WHO ARE THE COLLECTORS?

SOME people are natural collectors, and others are not, a true dichotomy because there is no halfway between the two. Either you are a born collector or you are not. Those who are not may acquire the taste. But it is as inborn to some people as being left-handed or stubborn or optimistic, or possessing red hair or a sense of humor. It shows up early. Take a little boy's pockets or a little girl's trinket box. Think back to the cigarette cards, arrowheads, butterflies, post cards, perfume bottles, toy animals of childhood days. Boys seem to be more natural collectors than girls for some reason. Often children outgrow the tendency to collect, but if it is inborn it survives to manifest itself later on. Hobbies may be discarded, but the instinct itself persists.

Collecting runs in families. Thus a famous collector of Wedgwood has a wife who collects blown glass, one son who goes in for coins, and another for stamps. There is in another family a fine collection of parasol and umbrella handles that has been passed down and added to for three generations. It is hardly a new habit. There have always been collectors of something. As far back as 1831 there was a series of prints caricaturing collectors of such things as shells, botanical specimens, china, etc. Over a hundred years ago an Englishman bewailed the "souvenir spoon collectors" who pilfered spoons from their hosts.

But there are degrees in this congregation of collectors. The lowest is the scavenger. He is the miser, the hoarder, the junkman, the otherwise normal person who will collect anything without rhyme or reason just for the sake of owning it. His fingers fairly itch to possess just for the sake of possession alone, not for any other values in what he collects. Psychologists call it the magpie complex. This pure scavengering may be partly explained by the fact that a scavenger can't bear to see anything go to waste. The result can be as extreme as the house of the Collyer brothers, the accumulation of trash carried away by the "penny man" at an auction—he's a ten-cent man now, his bidding has gone up—or as compulsive as the string-saving of the man who rolls up a ball larger than himself to exhibit on a TV show. It can also be as harmless and amusing as the habits of my good friend Cora, who calls herself a collector. Cora is a true scavenger, but she is not possessive, for she is just as ready to give away her spoils as to collect them. Perhaps thrift is her motivation. But if you want to get rid of something just call Cora. She'll take it and store it until someday it comes in handy for herself or for someone else. I don't know what she'd do if she had to live in small quarters.

Yes, Cora likes to think of herself as a collector. She is quite serious about it, pointing to her several collections all going at once, cups and saucers, dolls, bells, cookie cutters, and tin pieces "for painting sometime." Cora is interested in quantity rather than quality. Old, new, good, bad, or indifferent matters not to Cora. She likes to tell you that she has 53 dolls, 47 cups and saucers, 29 cookie cutters, and 61 bells. Needless to say she does not spend much on her collecting. Things come to her. She also has a good nose for smelling out a bargain at a rummage sale or a real find in a trash heap, a sense many a better collector might envy. But Cora has fun.

In reverse there is Mr. R. who goes in for pipe tampers, having narrowed down to these from his original collecting of tobacco antiques because tampers were harder to find. He likes to make it hard for himself. He won't admit anything into his collection unless it is older than a certain date that he has set for himself. He is a true collector of high caliber, and he has fun, too, in his way.

As we examine this love for collecting, whether inborn or acquired, we find it tied in closely with other traits, the curiosity of the explorer, the detective instinct for unraveling a mystery or defining the elusive, a liking for competition, and a pride in achieving. And most essential is a love for the things collected. The true collector is not one who puts no value on possessions or who believes in traveling light. He acquires things because he likes them and perhaps for what they stand for, whether it is old trade cards, Hester Bateman silver, Christmas tree lights, or Battersea enamels. It does not necessarily mean that he cannot be a spiritual person, but he certainly could not be an ascetic.

The collector is apt to have a one-track mind or at least he knows how to keep his enthusiasms on the beam. On top of it all he is a bit of a horse-trader. Collectors are hard bargainers once they have learned how to buy. They would have to be unless they have unlimited funds. They are very price-conscious. They like to crow about how little they paid for one thing, while they brag about how much it cost them to buy some rare piece they discovered ahead of the next fellow. But they support the antique business.

All in all the collector is an interesting personality as are most people with an all-absorbing hobby.

If you are a born collector the trait will out—like murder. You won't be able to conceal it or control it. You probably won't need any prodding. But if it is not a part of your natural make-up, the desire may still come by *accident*. This can happen through the acquiring, in some way not intentional, the beginnings of a collection. Aunt Lidie dies and leaves you a dozen Staffordshire cottages. For sentimental reasons you don't want to throw them out, give them away, or sell them. So you hold on to them wondering what to do with them. Then one day you read about these little ornaments in a book or magazine, or you see some in an exhibit, or a visitor raves about them, telling you how valuable they are, and you pick up interest. You buy the next one you see and the next, and you are off on the path to being a collector in your own right.

The same thing can happen with gifts. A friend is clearing out an old house and gives you some pieces of tea-leaf china. You see some more at a sale to match, and you begin to fill in your set. You realize that other people want it, too, and that it is a popular collectible. So, having made a good start, you decide to go on with it. Or perhaps you have twenty nice old silver spoons that your grandmother gave you as she gave all her grandchildren, one for each birthday. She has been dead some years, and the spoons are beginning to assume age and value. You decide to seek others to go with them and begin to get knowledgeable about old patterns and makers. You are a collector before you know it.

A collector of mustache cups, a man over fifty years of age, began his hobby years ago with a cup an uncle had brought him from Carlsbad, Bohemia, where he had gone to "take the cure." The little boy had kept the cup as a curiosity, and it was not until he was a grown man that he realized it was a relic of the days before men were clean shaven and was worth collecting as a hobby.

Or a collection may be started with a single piece picked up by accident at a sale or a shop just because you liked it or it excited your curiosity. It could be an odd piece of four glass balls, one on a base of three, a paperweight perhaps. You keep your eyes open and find another, this time with an inkwell on the base and of ruby glass. Then another of opalescent glass with a vase on top. Your interest is wide-awake. You are intrigued. You keep looking and asking, and your collection grows. You may even find that you are one of the few people in the country who have such a collection because this glass, though not particularly valuable, is rare.

Next there is the collector by contagion. Collecting can be catching. Someone you know collects trivets. You go along on the shopping trips for the ride, but before long you've got the fever, and because you don't want to compete with her you start picking up something else, say butter molds, under her supervision. It won't be long before you are on your own. In this class are the collectors who go in for something because everybody else is doing it, the faddists. Such a person does not want to be left out or considered behind the times when she goes along with the other "girls" on antiquing safaris. She wants a collection to show off and talk about, too. This is not a very strong basis on which to build a collection. When the first enthusiasm is over it is often forgotten. But sometimes it turns out very well. The collector's interest may not peter out but may possibly outstrip the others' as she awakens a slumbering curiosity she did not know she possessed.

Another collector we might call one by defense. This is usually the spouse of a confirmed collector who has to take to collecting on his own or be left at home and bored stiff. To-day the golf widow often has to move over and console the antiques widow or widower. When they do team up, a married pair may differ in their fervor or in the choice of things they collect—as far apart perhaps as bridle rosettes and lace fans—but their communal pilgrimages bring peace to the family and a meeting of interests.

There is another type of collector, the one who goes into it as a therapeutic hobby. His doctor orders him to do something absorbing enough to get his mind off his work or his ills, to release dangerous tensions, to avert a breakdown, etc. Collecting will fill the bill unless strenuous physical exercise is called for. Take the story of Mr. B, now an advanced collector. Fifteen years ago Mr. B, a manufacturer, was threatened with a serious breakdown. His business was in poor shape. His doctor ordered a general easing up, which Mr. B said was impossible. But he agreed to find some diversion. One day he followed his wife and sister-in-law into an antiques shop where the sister was looking for pattern glass. He had never been in an antiques shop before in his life. He kept picking up piece after piece, until he found in his hands an especially fine luster pitcher. It appealed to him. He bought it for what seemed then like a big price. Then he went home to find out what he had bought and why it was so expensive. The next week he started out looking for more luster. He was caught, off on his hobby before he knew it. Today he has not only a fine and extensive collection of all kinds of luster but side collections of historic blue, old tin, and carved birds. The house is full of his "junk," as Mrs. B called it at first. Their old friends can't understand it and think he is slightly touched. Many have stopped coming, but other different kinds of friends have taken their place. His wife is now resigned to the clutter because she knows that it saved her husband's sanity and probably his business, which he was able to hold on to because collecting helped him to meet his problems without panic. She is beginning to be convinced that it was money well spent, a good investment in dollars as well as in health, but she still shudders when he pays several hundred dollars for a piece of old Wedgwood. However, Mr. B goes on. There is no stopping him now.

For whatever reason one goes in for collecting there are certain basic qualifications a collector should have or he won't go far. First there should be interest. One can't go at this business apathetically. There are many whose interest does not lie deep enough to hold out for the acquiring of a sizable collection. It dies out. They get tired of lion glass after buying six pieces because it is hard to find. Or they start with carnival glass because it is cheaper and easy to find, but discover they don't really like it and come to a stop. After a few false starts they forget all about collecting. Interest in a collection should build as it grows and gets more specialized. It should increase in a ratio with the difficulty of finding things instead of dying off. This is the fun. A true collector will stop only when his collection gets topheavy. Then he may go on to something else or clean out the old one of less desirable pieces and go on again. There are some collectors so endowed with the zest for acquiring old things that they keep several collections going at once so that if availability lags in one area there is something else to turn to. Others find it helps to take on a partner to keep interests stimulated or to join a group of other enthusiasts.

The collector should have curiosity. Just buying another doll because you already have ten is not enough. You should know what you are buying and why, where it fits into the whole picture, why your doll has only part of a bisque scalp where others have a full molded head, and so on. Curiosity adds the zip to collecting. It sends the collector to libraries, books, magazines, lectures, and museums to find out. All this usually comes after the first more available pieces have been acquired. It may be the dividing line between the beginning and the advanced collector. A really advanced collector knows his field so thoroughly that he can often tell you exactly how many pieces of his collectible were made, how many are in existence, and where they are. Sometimes he makes a mistake, a happy one, like the man who collects mechanical banks and was assured that there were only nine of a certain model in existence. A bit of publicity in a newspaper smoked out two more. Now he has something to tell the older advanced collector who wrote the book about banks. Hereafter he will give his curiosity more rope. Another man who has not been at his collecting long has concentrated on napkin rings because they offer a challenge to his curiosity. Information on them is meager but he is not giving up. Someday he will be able to write a paper on napkin rings. A woman who collects glass finger bowls came upon a two-lipped one. It was sold to her as a finger bowl but she was dubious. It was some time until she found out what it really was, a wine basin, for cooling the wineglasses by hanging them over the lips of the bowl in cold water, just as wineglasses were cooled in the big *monteith* bowls with the scalloped edges, only this was for the individual table setting. The result of her curiosity has so fascinated her that she is starting a second collection of them.

The collector should have a *sense of good taste* and *discrimination*. In a very nice discussion of this subject at the beginning of her book *Antique Collecting for Everyone*, Katharine Morrison McClinton makes the statement that "the collector who arms himself with an appreciation of artistic values will never be cheated." She feels that beauty and evidence of artistic skill should come before historical or social value or even age. Many will agree with her. Unfortunately it would rule out many of the small collectibles that are available today and might keep many beginning collectors out of the field. It is a choice you will have to settle with yourself. If something ugly makes you shudder every time you look at it, better not buy it. If you can laugh at the decorated rolling pins and the plates run with ribbons and the souvenir glass from Atlantic City or Niagara Falls or grotesque bottle figures, go ahead and collect them and have your fun. But there is always a "best" in every area of collecting. Don't settle for anything less. Even in the "name brand" pieces, such as Queen Anne and Tiffany glass, there are good and bad examples. Here is where good taste, a feeling for line and form and color come in. It is well to be armed with a sense of discrimination before you even decide what you are going to collect.

The collector should have energy and the ability to organize time. You can't sit still and expect things to come to you. It often takes a lot of what newspapermen call legwork to track down collectibles, although it is possible, as will be shown later in this book, to do some of your buying by mail. Of course as you progress and your reputation as a collector of a certain thing gets around, people will notify you when they have something that might interest you or bring it to you or even give it to you. But this does not start or make a collection. You'll find the time you once gave to the movies or TV, to golf or social obligations, will be going toward seeking out new pieces to add to your collection. You will find yourself traveling miles just for one piece, sitting through endless sales, visiting ten shops until you find a thermometer worthy of buying. Of course the whole thing can be taken slowly and made compatible with your way of life, but collecting has a way of becoming compelling and absorbing if you are serious about it at all.

The collector should be able to budget. If your conscience is going to hurt every time you buy a new piece, if it is going to take the bread out of the mouths of your children, rob their penny banks, or put the household budget out of kilter, don't start. Even the smallest, most reasonable pieces are going to make holes in the pocketbook, and as for the more popular collectibles and the rarer pieces sums can get really astronomical. Many people have stopped collecting when they see what their choice takes in dollars and cents. Yet others go on and make it up by doing without something else. For this reason it is a good idea to consider the expense and pick on something you can afford to buy because once started there is no stopping the true collector from buying what he thinks he must have.

So there you are. You want to collect, you are interested in some particular class of antiques, you like mysteries and puzzles, you thrill to adventure and the excitement of the chase, you have good taste and a sense of discrimination to recognize the good from the bad, as much time and energy to devote to your collecting as you would to any hobby, and a bit of money you won't miss. Now how are you going to go about it? What are you going to collect and when should you begin? To find out, turn the page.

2.

HOW TO GET STARTED

IT IS easy enough to get started on a collecting career if you already have the nub of a collection, one perhaps inherited or given to you. If you like what you have, you keep on with it—provided that you can afford to buy in today's market. But even though prices may be high for what you buy now, consider that the average cost of your pieces in the long run will be considerably lower. It brings your investment down in case you want to dispose of it later. So if you have inherited your grandfather's pewter collection you would not be unwise to add to it.

Some people ease into collecting. They pick up a piece here and there with no definite ideas of adding to them. Then a friend says, "I have a piece of that majolica pattern. I'll give it to you," and this spurs another purchase, until gradually the few pieces assume collection proportion. And here is where the inevitable question is bound to be asked: "How many pieces do you have to have to make a collection?" It would be foolish to try to answer with any definite number. It is not a matter of quantity but of destination. If you have six fine fans and know you are going to collect more, I'd say you had a beginning collection. On the other hand, it might be hard to find six wheel-back Hepplewhite chairs even if you wanted to collect more. Every day you read of collections of glass or china that run into hundreds. In describing a collection the number of pieces is usually mentioned to give some idea of its importance. But it is quality and variety not size that really count. Most collectors do not go in for duplicates, unless they think they can turn them to advantage by selling or trading them. Duplicates might be kept by cautious collectors as "spares," especially if the piece is quite uncommon and hard to find. Making up sets, of course, is different. Most people aim for a dozen matching goblets, let's say, or plates, or silver settings. On the other hand, there is the man who collects cut-glass wineglasses and is aiming at only one of every known pattern made. Quite a project, but interesting.

If you are starting from scratch to collect, it might be well to pause and give some thought to what you want to get out of this collecting. On what basis will you select your items? Will it be mainly for beauty or decorative value, things you can display or even use with pride? Or for historical or social significance, choosing some period in which you are particularly interested such as the Civil War, late Victorian, or the settling of the Far West? Or for nostalgia or sentimental or romantic reasons, seeking out things you recognize or remember? Or to tie up with your profession or avocation or other hobby? Or perhaps items based on your name or birth year? Or for pure fun? There are lots of fun collections that have no other reason for being. Or just because you like it—as good a reason as any.

Your ideas may change as you go along. Maybe you won't have any definite basic idea when you start, but you'll find yourself leaning a certain way as you progress, and your collection will become more consistent and valuable. After all, if you are going to put out money for your antiques you might just as well keep an eye on their ultimate dollar value. If you are up in the air about a choice, do some reading. Look over the late numbers of magazines that have to do with antiques and hobbies. Watch what the dealers are advertising to get an idea of the things other collectors are asking for. If you are wise, you'll keep away from the things that are in most demand.

Probably the biggest problem with most of us is where the money is going to come from to buy the things we meet in this market of high prices. With your own income and resources in mind, you should give this serious consideration before you begin. If you are the patient kind who will be satisfied to pick up only a few pieces a year, you can afford to look into cameo glass or marked American pewter or Chinese import china. But if you like things to move fast, there are many interesting collectibles that can give lots of satisfaction although they cost very little because as separate items they are not worth much of anything. Take things such as buttons. Now there are, of course, many valuable buttons that go into dollars, but there are plenty to be bought for a few cents a piece. An old button string can be picked up for a reasonable sum and might yield several good collectible ones. Or take advertising cards, those quaint little bits of pasteboard that advertised soap or coffee or other commodities. Alone such a card is worthless except to a collector. You can get them for as little as 25 cents to $1.00 a piece.

For the budget-minded collector there are other things that won't mean a great outlay of money. These are the so-called antiques of the future, new things of the moment that may eventually fill out a collection as important as similar old things, or oddities reflecting the customs of the last twenty-five years or more which in another twenty-five will begin to be looked upon with respect because of age. Let's say you are interested in figural bottles, those glass or pottery containers made in human or other forms for liquor, perfume, medicine, bitters, etc. Many go back to the early 1800's. They are getting hard to find, and the prices are mounting. But there are figural bottles being made and used today. Many for advertising purposes, such as fancy liquor bottles. Why not go in for these? Get your friends to save them for you. Someday they'll be worth what you'd pay for the older ones today, and they're just as good to look at.

So here is a list of suggestions of some of the things you may find around in the shops that are still not in the high-price bracket.

Antiques of the Future

Current perfume bottles
Gibson girl items
Early comic books
Things made in Occupied Japan
Reissue figure bottles and new figural bottles
Reproduction spatter plates
Plated silver from 1900 on
Late dinnerware patterns
Calendar art
Chromos
Crayon portraits
Cigarette lighters
Cigarette cases
Vanities or compacts
Ration books

Ash trays—unusual ones
Tricky salts and peppers
Davy Crockett items
Space toys
Birchbark pictures
Fungus pictures
Burned wood pictures
Moss pictures
Patchwork pictures of cloth and tweeds
Cut leatherwork
Aviation items
Franklin Roosevelt items
General MacArthur items
Eisenhower items
Churchill items
Queen Elizabeth items
Decorative tin boxes
Advertising items
Catalogues
Souvenirs
Recent Tobies
Hummel figures
Quimper ware
Deruta ware
Costume jewelry
Wallace Nutting pictures
Maxfield Parrish prints
First and last numbers of defunct magazines
Newspapers recording some special event
Wine labels
Brass desk pieces
Embroidery

Crochet
Comic greeting cards
Christmas seals
Easter seals
College pennants
License plates

They may seem hardly worth the attention of the serious collector, but who would have bothered collecting Prang prints or cards fifty years ago? Mechanical banks were just trick penny savers for the children up to 1900, and many pressed-glass patterns were giveaways with baking powder or tea.

Perhaps the best way to settle this question of money for your collecting is to make a budget for yourself. Decide how much you should spend a year on your hobby and put yourself on an allowance. It may be only $10.00 a month and you may have to spend several months' allowance for some special piece. When you come upon something you can't afford to pass up, borrow from some other bracket in your budget, give up the new hat, the theater ticket, a dinner, or a special luncheon. If you are not prepared to do this, you better stick to still banks instead of mechanical ones, paper dolls rather than bisque dolls, later blue souvenir plates rather than Historic Blue Staffordshire, egg cups rather than covered animal dishes, and so on. You'll find you can save a lot, too, by buying unmarked pieces rather than marked ones. It may make your identification harder but it will go easier on the pocketbook. An unmarked pewter plate may cost $10.00 against a marked piece by Danforth for $35.00.

One woman of my acquaintance keeps a "penny jar" in which she drops coins she saves by making small sacrifices, walking instead of taking a taxi, doing her own hair, going without a dessert, resisting an impulse to buy a piece of costume jewelry she doesn't need. She uses these savings to buy the cheaper American paperweights that may run from $2.00 to $25.00. It gives her a virtuous feeling to finance her hobby in this way, and even though she has a mother to support on her salary, she has no pangs of conscience when she surveys her collection.

Instead of taking an expensive vacation at a resort, another thrifty woman corrals a friend with collecting habits to share the expenses of an auto trip through some part of the country that has a concentration of antiques. They travel as cheaply as possible, stay at modest motels, eat their lunch picnic fashion, and spend the rest of the vacation allowance on their finds.

A way to look at the cash expenditures for your collecting is as you would consider any hobby. Collecting may not add up to any more money than you would spend for photographic equipment, paint and canvases, dues and expenses for golf, or a night a week of bowling. Moreover, you should have something to show for your money that will not decrease in value or fade away.

It is easy to let spending get out of hand in one's first fervor. Take your time. Don't rush into this collecting business. The best collections, like Rome, were not built in a day. Don't buy the first thing you see or the first time you see it. The temptation is to buy today because it might not be there tomorrow. Maybe you are taking a gamble if you pass it up. Maybe it would be a different kind of gamble if you bought it. Consider. Bargain. If you have doubts, risk a small deposit on the piece. It is better to lose that than make a big mistake. Taking it slowly eases the money problem because you won't buy too much too quickly. The nice thing about collecting is that you can go as slowly or as fast as you like.

So keep in mind three things as you start to buy: go slowly and feel your way; keep your head and watch the budget; and select the best your money can buy. Don't compromise. But when you see a piece you are sure is right, don't let it get away. You'll never forgive yourself if you do.

3.

WHAT TO COLLECT

AS has been indicated in this book, the selection of the thing you intend to collect is very important. Unless it has been already selected for you by some happenstance it will be up to you to pick the thing you are going to set out to look for. Collecting of almost anything begins with a search. One doesn't just walk into a shop and say, "I'll take that." It might be the tenth shop you visit that will have the thing you want. But of course that is the fun, and as you advance into the mazes of collecting it will get harder and harder. The difference between beginning collecting and advanced search is the difference between taking a Cook's tour in Europe and a personal safari into the unexplored regions of the Andes. So let's see what these mazes have already yielded to the zealous pursuer and will yield to you.

It has been said that there is a collector for everything. This is probably true. A dealer in antiques must often wonder why people buy what they do. The only answer is that they are collectors, and every dealer thanks heaven for such customers for absorbing what might lie on his shelves for years or forever. Who would want an old cherry-stoner or a china nestegg but a collector? Or who would buy a faded wreath of dried flowers under glass except a collector of Victoriana?

The statement has been made that there are at least five hundred collectibles to be found in the antique market. It will be even more if you extend the word antique to include things made or used fifty years ago. Someone has defined the age of antiques into three periods: the first takes in anything made up to 1830, the date set by the United States Customs as a requisite for determining duty-free antiques, a date adhered to by the purists; the second is the period from 1830 to 1891, the year when the McKinley Act required that the country of origin be stamped upon the imported articles; and the third concerns simply the "old and pretty" things, from 1891 to any date you choose to set. Pre-1830 articles would be a discouraging limit for a beginner to set for himself, but there are many fine things for collecting in the second period that are one hundred years old, many closer to seventy or eighty. In fact, all the art glass so avidly collected now is just about seventy-five years old, some not that. In the third period belong what we call "the antiques of tomorrow," easily found pieces that are still fun to collect and worth treasuring.

But even with the wide scope allowed by age and variety it may still not be easy to settle upon just the right thing to collect because so many things will dictate your choice. The person who says, "I want to collect something but I don't know what," is really like a child with a nickel (it used to be a penny) at a candy counter. There are, however, some basic things to consider. Pick something you *like* even if it is not particularly unusual or will make snappy conversation. But if you have never done any collecting it is a good idea to start with something that is not too popular with other collectors at the moment. The minute anything comes to be talked about as a collectible the market is quickly bought up and it zooms in price.

Take mechanical banks. Not too long ago, not even ten years back, mechanical banks could be found in almost any shop and bought for a few dollars. Then the collectors got busy, and the specialists began to write about them and classify them according to rarity, and now the cheapest ones, if you can find them, run into money. It is always hard to explain why things as unattractive as this become popular but it might be because these banks offered the men a new collectible with a certain masculine interest and a chance to fool around with ingenious mechanism.

Or consider pattern glass once a "give-away" item with tea or baking powder. This fad got under way among the "girls" less than twenty-five years ago. Everyone started getting on the pattern-glass wagon. Then you could still find the older and better patterns in flint and soda glass such as Ashburton, Argus, Daisy and Button, Bellflower, etc., with goblets running about $2.00 a piece. Today these are rarities on the market, with goblet prices running $10.00 to $12.00 a piece and the "girls" have had to move on to later patterns if they insist on collecting in this area. So if the beginner really likes and wants pattern glass, she had better choose a later pattern —at least as a starter. What is more, she will be less apt to be confused with reproductions. It is well for the beginner to keep away from anything that has been widely reproduced. The more popular a collectible, the sooner a reproduction appears on the market.

If you are determined to collect pattern glass, it might be well to invest in one or more of the guidebooks, such as Ruth Webb Lee's books; the 5th edition of *Antiques and Their*

Current Prices, by Edwin Warman; Minnie Kamm's *Pitcher Books;* Millard's *Goblets;* the pattern-glass guide, by Alice Hulett Metz; and the most recent one, a check list by M. Ray Doubles, which has an alphabetical listing of 2,465 patterns and variants with the overlapping names mentioned in all the other books. In some cases reproductions are recorded as warnings for the uninitiated.

On the other hand, it is not encouraging to pick upon something to collect that is so unusual or rare that it can scarcely be found, like pinpricked pictures, for instance, or crab-footed spoons. This can happen when the beginning collector narrows down the area of his collecting too much. A larger category, one that might include pinpricked pictures with other handwork or the spoons with pewter or spoons generally, would be better.

If you have no ideas of your own to spark your search, talk to dealers or other collectors. They know better than anyone else what things are being asked for in the shops and can steer you away from or toward the right thing. For instance, only a few years ago a dealer said to me, "Why don't you start collecting card cases? Nobody has got on to them yet." He had several nice ones, but as I was not thinking of collecting anything at the time I turned down his advice. Now I wish I had taken it, considering the growing popularity of card cases. Take children's mugs, the tiny ones showing the mottoes, names, and transfer pictures of children at play. I've always been attracted to them, but now that I really covet them I find them costing at least $8.00 a piece, many more. I'm sure a famous collection of 1,200 mugs, including lusters, Leeds, Bristol, and all the Staffordshire makers would never have been assembled now at these prices. So if you decide to break into a bracket that has been pretty well covered, make up your mind that it may be costly but set yourself a top price and stick to it. It may mean more looking but you'll find there are still bargains in hiding.

One way of overcoming the handicaps in selecting a popular collectible is to select a cheaper and more available version of it. Perhaps you like paperweights, but you know you can never afford the expensive French ones such as Baccarat, St. Louis, or Clichy, where a small faceted weight no larger than a quarter can sell for $3,000, or even weights made at Sandwich, Massachusetts. But there are many interesting weights running from $5.00 to $25.00, so begin here.

Many collectible items are by their very nature cheaper to pick up, such as small sewing items, thimbles, sewing birds, pincushions, bodkins, etc., or the paper items such as post cards, greeting cards, posters, programs, newspapers, paper dolls, etc. Buttons can become very involved and run into money, but a good collection can get going on almost nothing.

Picking a category with a wide scope but an unusual angle makes a good starting point. If you choose a specific period such as the Regency, Victorian, Civil War, the Gay Ninetics, or the Dizzy Twenties, for instance, you will find yourself confronted with many byways of choice. Or if you choose to collect items concerning some personage you admire, you may be carried into the areas of glass, china, prints, and other categories. Or keep to symbols or motifs such as hands, roosters, the American flag, etc. One fine basis of classification is to select the antiques of your trade or profession. Your interest and specialized knowledge should be a great help in tracing down the old things. Thus one innkeeper buys up every liquor bottle put out before the law required that empty bottles should be broken so they could not be reused illegally—a ruling brought on by prohibition. A writer collects inkwells, a doctor old medicine bottles, a barber old razors. Commercial concerns do this sort of thing, and much valuable Americana has been preserved in their extensive collections.

I have tried to keep these various suggestions in mind as I made up the list that you will find at the end of this book. Of course it is not complete, it couldn't be, because there will always be collectors with new ideas and new angles on the old ones, but I have tried to cover the field with suggestions that I hope will inspire beginners to explore or from which to start on more original treks of their own. In making up this list I have kept the beginning collector in the front of my mind and for this reason I have not included many obvious areas of collecting which the beginner would not aspire to unless he already had some experience with antiques in a general way, or perhaps a few good pieces already in his possession by gift or inheritance. So if you don't find Stiegel or South Jersey glass, for instance, listed under No. 3, Glass, it is because I feel they are over the heads of the beginners. Of course there is no law to stop the beginner from starting at the top if he wants to, but considering the amount of money at stake, the knowledge required, and the difficulty in finding the older and rarer pieces that have escaped the museums, it would be foolhardy. It is much better for him to cut his teeth, as it were, on late nineteenth-century glass or silver souvenir spoons instead of Georgian silver, until he learns his way around the mazes of collecting.

On the other hand, it is not wise to pretend that such things do not exist. Even if you cannot collect them yourself, an interest and knowledge in all collectibles in your field are fine things to have so that you can keep things in perspective, and if the time comes when you are in a position to advance further and store up the finer things you will be ready for it. No collector can afford to be cloistered in his own little bracket. He should keep abreast of things in the antique world, read the magazines, follow the new books, study the pictures in the ads for the fine marked pewter pieces, the Queen Anne furniture, Chelsea china, Meissen figures, French tole, and so on. At least he learns to recognize what he cannot have. No collector can afford to dismiss the museums and the large collections as part of the education that will perhaps change his status from beginning to advanced collector.

It may seem that things have been included in the list at the back of the book that are slightly ridiculous, and as single items they might well be. But gathered into collections with a reason behind them, they take on meaning and stature. I am referring to things such as left-handed items, eye cups, or dish lids, yet someone has collected them for fun perhaps or for other personal reasons and has made interesting displays of them.

Another thing to keep in mind when reading through this list is that some things do not seem to be physically collectible unless you live in a barn or a museum. What would you do with twenty or thirty inn signs if you could find them? Still, there are people living in limited space who do collect cumbersome things such as cigar-store Indians, merry-go-round animals, cannons, figureheads, and old signs. So such things are included, too.

In most of the categories into which the list has been divided collecting can be done in one of two ways, generally, which covers the whole field, or narrowed down to one item. In some of the larger categories, such as glass, china, buttons, dolls, etc., general collecting does not hold the stimulus that narrowing down to one item would. This is why many items in the list are duplicated, as they fall into various categories, and why I have listed the available pieces in each class. Thus under silver you might find tea caddies, which would make a collection by themselves. But you'll also find caddies under wood, china, pewter, etc., and as they are popular collectibles, I have assembled them all in a category by themselves.

As an indication of popularity, I have put an asterisk against the two hundred most-sought-after collectibles which fall into the two following lists, both significant from two different angles. The first is based on figures given me by *Spinning Wheel,* one of the truly important magazines in the antique field, as the most active collective areas over a range of years. The list is quite general, as you can see.

1. Glass
2. China
3. Furniture
4. Dolls and toys
5. Buttons
6. Lamps
7. Clocks
8. Silver
9. Primitive or industrial items
10. Guns

The second is a list of the ten most popular current wants based on opinions given me by a poll of many dealers. There is not too much difference except that the second is more specialized and the order of preference is not the same.

1. Primitives
2. Guns
3. Banks
4. Pressed glass
5. Art glass
6. Pewter
7. Dolls and toys
8. Deep-colored ironstone (gaudy patterns)
9. Buttons
10. Luster

Looking over the large list at the back of the book and with an eye on the beginner, I feel some further explanations are in order. Under Furniture, No. 1, I have included only the smaller pieces that can be found in late as well as early periods. Where the advanced collector might go in exclusively for Queen Anne pieces or for Adam or Regency, the beginner would scarcely consider pieces of one period alone. Nor would he concentrate on large pieces such as cupboards or beds or even armchairs. If his taste runs to furniture, he will do his collecting in a different way, let's say by selecting Victorian pieces or country pieces or by collecting one item such as small stands or stools that can be fit into his décor without being overwhelming.

When it comes to silver, the early English and American pieces up to 1825 are omitted. Prices here are prohibitive. What you would pay for one Georgian teapot would start you out in fine fashion on the road to collecting silver napkin rings or coin silver spoons or salt cellars of the later 1800's.

Fine old Sheffield is not cheap either, but there are enough small pieces which would not be beyond the buying power of the beginner or could be included with pieces from other categories, such as inkstands, salts, wire baskets, sugars, candlesticks, and cruet stands. The epergnes, tea urns, wine buckets, etc., can be left for the advanced enthusiasts.

In glass, No. 3, except for the Lacy Glass cup plates of Sandwich and Midwestern factories, suggestions have been limited to the later glass of the 1800's. There is still plenty of choice here for good pieces without giving a thought to Stiegel, Amelung, Blown Three-Mold, English Nailsea, Bristol, Irish Waterford, Venetian, Baccarat, or German enameled glass. If bottles are the beginning collector's choice, he will find plenty of good pickings without going in for things such as the early "sealed" wine bottles with the seal impressed on the side, or South Jersey "seahorse" perfume bottles.

It almost seems as if dates were the dividing line between collectible items for beginning and advanced collectors, and it is easy to see why. The older things are the rarer they are and the more expensive. Also it takes more know-how to recognize an old piece, translate its markings, trace its maker, determine its use, and the date of its manufacture. A mistake here is costly. This is particularly true of china. It has been said that china collecting is not an avocation but a profession requiring continuous study. Anyone who goes in for it seriously should be prepared to give it much thought and research. That is why most of the early English china, both the soft-paste and the later porcelains and bone china, will not be included in the No. 4 list of china, even though they were imported and used here in America, who produced little early china of its own. All the familiar English names such as Chelsea, Bow, Derby, Worcester, Lowestoft, Leeds, Minton, Spode, Salopian, Pratt, Swansea, Sunderland, Caughley-Coalport-Ridgway, Jackfield, Elers, Davenport, Bristol, Lambeth,

Delft, Wedgwood, and Whieldon have formed the background of many famous collections. The same can be said for Irish Belleek; Meissen and Dresden from Germany; Sèvres and Mennency from France; Faïence and Capo-di-Monte from Italy; Delft from Holland; and Royal Copenhagen from Denmark. All these as well as such oriental imports as Imari, Satsuma, Canton, true Celadon, and even the popular Chinese export China (misnamed Oriental Lowestoft), will not greatly concern the beginner. However, included in the list are many other imports aimed at the American market in the early 1800's which because of popularity, availability, and easily determined identity could be investigated by the beginning collector even though the prices often run high, as in Gaudy Dutch and Spatter. These are listed as suggestions for the daring ones. It would be too bad to suggest that the beginning collector should consider only less interesting pieces from the later Victorian era.

Among the brass pieces—No. 13—listed for collectors again, it is well to remember that the early brass in America was mostly imported and that such things as elaborate chandeliers, early period styles in candlesticks, clock dials, and period andirons may be out of bounds for the beginner.

When it comes to clocks and watches—No. 18—the beginner will take it easy as he gets into the earlier pieces. Buying such a thing as a tall-case or grandfather's clock would be a matter of importance in most families, although a fine clock passed down in the family might form the core for a collector who wants to go in for clocks of all kinds. Certainly he is not going to buy extensively in the early brackets. He will be more apt to start with more available things and move slowly. Most clock collectors become advanced in their status very soon, or at least as soon as they can afford the better things. Even if they go in for novelties rather than the works of the early makers, they will soon learn to talk glibly about them. The same thing holds for watches, although a very interesting collection can be made of watches that are not too old or novel.

About the No. 20 classification, coronation and commemorative pieces, it should be stated again that although there are many interesting English coronation pieces in glass, pottery, china, and metal that could include such outstanding things as Blue-Dash chargers showing the heads of William and Mary, the Boscobel Oak plate of Liverpool Delft (Charles II), and other pieces right through Queen Charlotte and Queen Victoria to the mementoes of the reigning Queen Elizabeth II, there are many other things of a commemorative nature to reward the beginner, even leaving out of consideration the more valuable American presentation pieces of silver, glass, and china.

There is a fascination in old clothing and costumes—No. 21— and the beginning collector will have a good time feeling his way around this field. If he is interested, he will never let an old piece of wearing apparel get by him, or even old costume accessories. The competition here is not too keen except in certain items, because many people don't know what to do with old costumes except keep them in a trunk. But the collector can do a real service if he makes himself a repository for such things to be lent to theatrical productions or pageants. One woman in a small town with a big stock of old clothes, early and late, inherited or given her by friends, is known as a source for fashion shows, amateur plays, and school projects. She is a real asset to the community.

Dolls—No. 23—offer one of the most popular and easiest of collectible fields to get into. A collector may start small but with so many books, clubs, and museums to widen his knowledge he won't stay a beginner for long. Many doll collectors are not discriminating. They will mix the new with the old, the foreign, souvenir, and costume dolls with more important items. This is up to the individual. But the collector of antique dolls will find the search more exciting the more he limits his buying and the more he learns about old dolls.

Enamels are suggested among the collectibles in No. 25 because they do have a fascination for many people. Although things such as Battersea and even Staffordshire might fall beyond the limit of beginning buyers as a class, there are certain pieces still not too prohibitive to be included in a collection. If I were collecting enameled wares I would certainly hope to include at least one piece of Fabergé, the work of the famous Russian goldsmith of the 1870's. Indeed this might be a good rule to follow for any beginner, to allow himself the luxury of one very fine piece in his category to spike his collection.

If your taste runs to figurines and figure ornaments—No. 26—you have plenty of choice without going into Meissen, Chelsea, or Ming, although there is nothing to stop the beginner if he covets a fine piece. But for specialization the lower brackets are better. Beware of reproductions here. A lot of imported trash is being brought into this country to bewilder the beginner without much knowledge.

When it comes to firearms—No. 27—the beginner enters a highly specialized field. But most men are undaunted. Even small boys begin to talk gun language very young. You see them at sales holding their own against more experienced buyers. They learn fast. Many books have been written on firearms, and the purchase of several with price lists might save the collector a costly mistake.

Volumes have also been written about old iron stoves and hardware—No. 32—so there is no excuse for the beginner to make mistakes in this field. In fact, he is fairly safe in picking up any piece of old iron as soon as he has learned the signs of age, the pitting, color, weight, etc. Just because a piece of iron is rusty does not mean that it is old. Reproductions are treated that way to fool buyers. This is a rewarding hobby, as there is still plenty of old iron around although the field is being drained by collectors. As for the Victorian cast-iron pieces, they are legion.

Unless the collector is aiming to build up a collection covering the whole history of lighting in America—No. 39— he will probably pass by the earlier things such as rushlights and Betty lamps and fat lamps and specialize on other things. It is a vast subject with something for everyone in it right up to the collecting of early electric-light bulbs. Two of the most popular items are miniature lamps and fairy lamps, both available but getting expensive.

The same thing holds for mirrors—No. 44—as for furniture. One good piece might be bought for the home, but a fine old mirror in Queen Anne, Chippendale, or Federal period styles runs high and one is not apt to buy a dozen of them. But there are quite a few things in the mirror bracket that could interest the beginner who likes mirrors. The same words could practically be used for musical instruments— No. 46. No one except a museum or a commercial concern is going to collect pianos, spinets, or organs. But a single interesting buy in this line might start a general collection of musical instruments. In fact, this is a wide field, and many items are collected exclusively, such as music boxes or old phonographs. That there is a national society for such col-

lectors shows how widespread this hobby is. It is a good one
for the beginner to look into.

In the art category that embraces paintings and prints—No.
51—the beginner will have to tread carefully. He would
scarcely start collecting primitive portraits or paintings or
miniatures or even early silhouettes unless he already had
some specialized knowledge or the beginning of such a collection and a reason for it, like one collector I know who
is a descendant of Ruth Bascom, the New England portrait
painter of the early 1800's and possesses a number of Bascom
portraits. Naturally she would be interested in collecting
more. But there are plenty of opportunities to specialize in
the earlier aspects of American art for interested collectors.
Reading and study are indicated in almost every bracket of
this field.

Pewter—No. 53—is something to approach with awe. So
much depends here on a knowledge of marks and makers in
both the English and American pewter that it is more for the
advanced collector than for the beginner. There is, however,
a lot of unmarked pewter around, and if you like it, collect
it. You may be buying britannia, however, which does not
matter if you can recognize it. Britannia was made by many
of the pewterers in the first half of the 1800's. It was spun and
not molded and the percentage of the alloys differed, but it,
too, has its marks which it would be a good idea to know
before you begin browsing in the pewter field. Learn to recognize the modern pewter as opposed to the old.

With such warnings I hope the reader who contemplates
starting a collection will not make a false start. It is discouraging to pick a collectible that one very soon finds is too
expensive to follow up, so rare that it is hard to find, too hard
to recognize. I hope I have cleared things up and sifted out

or at least tagged the more available and "safe" items that will lure the beginner into the fold. I hope in the long appended list there will be an answer for everyone who says, "I want to collect something but I don't know what to collect."

4.

WHERE TO FIND COLLECTIBLES

A COLLECTION is not assembled without time, a sense of adventure, and money. It is not put together overnight. If it were, there would be no fun in it. Few people would care to go out and buy a collection intact unless it were a small one to which they hoped to add. The thing that gives collecting its attraction and excitement is the chase. Tracking down the elusive things you know exist somewhere, coming unexpectedly upon those you never heard of, is more than half the satisfaction even for the beginning collector. To do this means, of course, that you must put yourself in contact with places and people who deal in your chosen specialty.

The most obvious way is to haunt the antique shops, but it is not the only way. If you live in an area where such shops are fairly numerous, this is not too much of a project. It's a wonderful excuse for a day off to go "antiquing." Get together a car, four informed friends each with her own specialty to be hunted, each with a few dollars that won't be missed, map an itinerary of an unplumbed area with plenty of shops close together, and you come up with an experience that is not only as much fun as a matinee in town or an afternoon of bridge but is often more profitable. It is also a fine objective for the family outing on weekends or holidays. Antiquing has become a national pastime.

Your success in the shops will vary. You may not be in the right part of the country for what you want. If it is a popular item, like Mary Gregory glass or Imari ironstone, you may have to look long and often, search out shops off the beaten track, go farther afield in your antique travels. Vacation trips offer fine opportunities for finding things not available nearer home. They widen the horizon of your search and up the chances of your finding what you want. People who travel in their business or profession can use their wanderings to advantage. There is the man who travels for a utility company and gets into many homes where he often spots antiques that can be bought. There is also the wife of an engineer who goes with him when he makes his cross-country trips and thus is able to visit new shops to pick up new and different cruets and art glass to add to her collections. While he works, she antiques, and everybody is happy.

Every collector should make an effort to know the specialists among the dealers. This knowledge will come with experience, from shop talk, chatting with dealers, or by reading the ads in the magazines devoted to antiques. You might say that there are two kinds of dealers in antiques, those who go in entirely or heavily for certain things such as pressed glass, art glass, primitives, Oriental Lowestoft, guns, pewter, etc. Maybe their business began with a collection of their own or with one they purchased as a starter. They have spent time in research and through study and comparison have become more or less knowledgeable in their specialty. Usually these dealers are the older ones in the business who have developed along the lines that interest them most, or on things more available in their area or which are better money-makers. They have had time to build up a stock of special items.

Then there is the other kind of dealer who sells everything, some good things, some not so good, depending upon what he can find to sell—a problem with most dealers today. He may prefer this kind of birdshot dealing better than the other. He has something to offer everybody. His eggs are in many baskets. That does not mean that his personal interests are as wide as his stock. He may be a collector himself. You'd be surprised how many dealers do collect things they do not sell. Sometimes it is a canny way of laying up a stock against a higher market, but often it is just for the same reasons that other people collect. Often this second type of dealer, if he is a comparative newcomer in the business, will have a great variety of things that might have been called junk a few years back. His shop may be only a step up from the old secondhand shop but it is here that you may find many of the cheaper, newer collectibles, the undiscovered pieces that will be popular when the news gets around that collectors are after them, the almost-antiques of tomorrow.

But no matter what the shop (except for the absolute specialists) a visit is always like opening a prize package in a raffle. You never know what will turn up. So you become a "looker," a breed that many dealers despise, but the wiser ones suffer, knowing full well that many a looker will surprise them by becoming a good buyer. You browse around and tucked in a corner behind the cut glass you may find an unusual knife rest in silver plate, or a quaint pencil box. In a tray of odds and ends you may find an old watch chain slide or spot an old hymnal in a heap of sad-looking books. And just when you've given up hope of ever finding another of the Literary Series of Clews plates there it stands in a dark corner of a cupboard.

It is well to establish confidence in a dealer by asking for what you want, though some collectors feel this immediately gives the dealer the edge in the bargaining. Better to "discover" it and ask about the price casually, they say. But don't fool yourself. Dealers know all the tricks. And don't count on the ignorance of a dealer. It is surprising how knowledgeable they are considering the amount of material they handle. They may not know as much about your specialty as you do who have given it study but they do know the popular collectibles and they are not going to hide a pack of old playing cards in a box of paper junk. Nobody knows more about what is being collected than the dealers. News travels fast among them. Their business is being supported by the flood of collectors of everything from luster to Rookwood pottery.

And so there should be an advantage in knowing what you want when you enter a shop. It takes you out of the casual looker class and gives the dealer the idea that you might be a serious buyer. If he doesn't have what you ask for, at least he is inclined to talk about it, tell you where you might find it, or offer to get it for you. If you happen to strike a shop where you feel the dealer does not know his stock, a very few don't, it may pay you to look around for yourself. But as a rule your question will get a prompt and definite answer.

One of the best ways to pick up your collectible is to make friends with the dealers, maybe just one or maybe several. Pop in and out of their shops until you are a familiar caller, but be careful not to become a nuisance. Talk shop if they seem so inclined. Show that you know something about what you're looking for. You may even be able to tell *him* something. Many a dealer acknowledges that he learns a lot from his customers. Buy something occasionally even if it is not the thing you're collecting. Ask him to make a note of your wants and keep you in mind when he finds what you are looking for. Be specific. Describe what you *don't* want if it is already in your collection. Don't rely on a dealer's memory. You are only one of many who come into the shop asking for things. A good dealer, however, will be able to sort out his customers or keep a record of their wants in a book for the purpose. Then when he sees a majolica tobacco jar he will not have to say to himself, "Let's see, who is it is looking for tobacco jars?" but will go to his record and find your name. Of course the more important you become as a collector the better you will be remembered.

It will expedite matters for both you and the dealer if you leave with him a few self-addressed post cards or stamped envelopes which can be slipped into the mail with little effort. A busy dealer is apt to forget and will put off writing or phoning you. Most antique businesses are not set up with office help to take care of correspondence in a big way. The very nature of the business, which is often run under the home roof as an auxiliary activity, would bear out the statement that antique dealers are not always businesslike people. Perhaps they are closer to the arts than to commerce. So make it easy for them.

The next easiest way to look for your antique collectibles is to visit the antiques shows and fairs. Here you have the advantage of covering twenty to fifty exhibitors in one visit. It gives you a chance to make new dealer friends from your own locality or from a distance if it is a big show, and to do a bit of comparative looking and shopping. Don't be content just to browse, but make a point of asking questions even if you do not see what you want. A dealer can bring only a small portion of his stock with him and he might very well have just what you want at home in his shop.

Auctions and sales still bring many antiques out of hiding and it pays to go to as many as you can. If there is an opportunity of seeing beforehand what will be auctioned off, so much the better. At country sales, if you go early, you will have a chance to look things over, dig in the boxes, open drawers, examine the tables of things set out to be sold. Sometimes it seems hardly worth-while to stand all morning or afternoon for the one piece you want to be put up. But if you know the ropes, you can get around this. Ask the auctioneer or his helper to put the piece up before he comes to it, or I've often seen a canny bidder quietly slip a piece close to the auctioneer's hand so that it will be put up without waiting its turn. I've even seen a bidder slip a good piece into a box of trash, or a good plate in a pile of common ones in the hope that it won't be noticed and he'll get the whole thing very cheap without any competitive bidding. Keep your eyes open at a sale. And if you don't want to wait for some special piece leave your bid with a friend who is going to sit it out to the end.

It is possible in many big sales to post your bid beforehand. In the foreword of a catalogue put out for a sale by a big auction room you may find these words: *Bids will be accepted and executed without charge.* Also the exhibition day or days for viewing the articles to be sold are usually stated. If you know your prices and have an idea of how high you will go even with competition, you can set your limit and leave your bid. The disadvantage of this is that you have committed yourself and if you were present you might find that you might want to go higher or be lucky enough with a lower bid to get it more cheaply. Of course in a well-conducted auction the auctioneer can do the latter for you, but with your higher limit as a lever he could use it to provoke higher bidding.

Many of the big city galleries and the big auction rooms across the country where advertised sales are put on, regularly issue catalogues, often illustrated. Sometimes you will have to pay for such a catalogue, but it is well worth it, as it gives you a chance to study at leisure and in advance what will be offered for sale. It is well to get on the mailing lists of those auctioneers and galleries that send out notices of sales to come. It is in such places that collections are sold off and estates converted into cash. This is where the better collectibles come on the market again and where the collectors gather like vultures at a feast. Because the pieces may be rare, if they've been held for some time, and because such an opportunity to purchase comes very seldom, prices are apt to be high. This rule, however, can be unexpectedly broken for a number of reasons. So don't stay away just because you feel sure you can't compete with other buyers. You might be surprised. It is possible that too many things might be put on the market at once and thus water the demand. Often large collections are not sold all at once. Take the recent Arthur Sussel sale at the Parke-Bernet Galleries in New York, sold in three sessions months apart. Everyone in the business and collectors all over the country knew the fine collections of primitives and other antiques that this Philadelphia dealer had accumulated over the years. They were on their toes. Prices were high but the market absorbed it all because the sale was cleverly managed.

If you, a beginning collector, had sat in on this sale, you might not have bought a single thing, but you would have learned a lot perhaps about your own specialty or just antiques in general. If you do go to a sale like this, keep the catalogue in your hand and make marginal notes as well as prices. It will be a good reference for you in the future, even if you never become an advanced collector. This is how confirmed collectors keep track of the things they are interested in, where they are, who is in the market, etc., etc.

Another source of good collectible material is when museums sell off, as they occasionally do. This may be for several reasons. They may get overcrowded with no place to store the things that have been left to them or they may have duplicates they do not need. What has happened in some cases is that they are overstocked with pieces that were easy and cheap to acquire when the museum was being organized, and they don't need them all. Or the nature of the museum may change. They are more likely to dispose of these things through a professional auctioneer than privately. One auctioneer told me he had been called in by "an institution" to weed out some of the collections and work the pieces into some of his future sales. So here, too, is an opportunity for the collector to find things long since lost to the general market.

If you are a collector, don't hide your hobby under a bushel of anonymity. Advertise the fact. Tell your friends. Tell your acquaintances, the places where you shop, your business associates. Tell the world! Every interested friend is a scout and jumps at the chance to tell you when he finds something you are collecting. He may even buy it for you. No one is ever at a loss to know what to give a collector. He is definitely *not* the man who has everything. Everyone has a touch of the collector in him, and though it may not be strong enough to send him out collecting on his own he will love to enjoy the chase vicariously through his friends. A woman I know who is notoriously cautious with her money got so excited at finding a silver luster Toby jug on a vacation trip that she bought it—at a stiff price—and *gave* it to her lawyer just because she knew he collected Tobies. She would have looked twice, three times, at the money if it had been for anything else.

Another wise move for the collector is to join some kind of collecting group, either a local club of eager antiquarians, a branch of a national organization for those interested in antiques generally, such as the Questers, or a society devoted entirely to the thing he is interested in. There are many such groups. A list of them will be given at the end of this book. You will have the advantage of talking shop at meetings, get their literature and publications, and the chance to buy from or swap with other members—a big way of getting variety into your collection. In a group where everyone is collecting something different there are still mutual interests and cooperation between members.

Next to this free advertising of your hobby is paid advertising. It may pay you to insert a small ad more or less regularly in the wanted columns of your favorite antique magazine or your local paper. A man I know who has a large collection of coin glass does that. He may go months without a response, but when one comes it is worth the waiting and the expense.

Shopping by Mail

This is such an important way of buying antiques that it deserves a discussion all to itself. Armchair shopping or buying by remote control is becoming more and more popular with both sellers and buyers. This is owing to several things. First the collector knows what he wants. He isn't picking up odds and ends here and there. Again the growth in circulation of the magazines devoted to antiques where the ads for specific items appear (with consequently more advertising pages to lure the growing numbers of collectors) has a lot to do with it. This mail-order shopping is an especially convenient method for those confined to their homes who have no opportunity to make the rounds of the shops, shows, and sales. There is no doubt that it saves time, energy, gas, and carfare. It enlarges the scope of the market just like traveling.

There are dealers who do a large percentage of their business by mail. Some deal entirely by mail. They are set up to take care of the details of correspondence, billing, bookkeeping, etc. Some combine it with a shop business, some with merely exhibiting at shows as a way of getting publicity and new customers.

It is easily seen that it can be a "touchy" kind of business with many reasons for complaint on both sides. But over the years the disadvantages are being ironed out and certain codes established. It is only occasionally that unpleasant things happen to turn the public away from the dealers who sell by mail.

There is an advantage on both sides for this kind of buying. It releases a dealer from long hours of tedious shopkeeping, trying to be pleasant to people who take up his time and buy nothing. A shop can be a ball and chain unless there is someone to share the work. Some dealers get around this by advertising *By appointment only.* They are more apt to be the established ones who can afford to be independent of transient trade. From the viewpoint of the buyer it is discouraging to find a shop closed on a first visit. Shopping by mail does away with this hazard.

Where will you find the dealers who sell by mail? Their ads appear in every antique magazine, often with lists of specific items and the prices asked. What are your chances of getting these articles with hundreds, maybe thousands of other readers seeing the same things? That is the risk, but it can be minimized if you follow a few sensible rules:

1. Act immediately, don't wait to query if you feel the article is what you want. Send your check with enough to cover postage and send airmail or at least special delivery. It might even pay you to phone or wire.

2. If you have doubts or questions about pattern, color, size, condition, etc., send a query but *include a self-addressed, stamped envelope for reply.*

3. Or you can ask that the article be *sent on approval.* But if you do, send your check anyway. If the dealer does not believe in approval sales, he can return your check if a stamped envelope for reply is enclosed. Approvals are generally limited to seven to ten days. If you don't like what you get, send it back promptly. After all, you are depriving the dealer of a possible sale while it is out of the shop. Be very sure it is packed carefully, and if you carry no insurance with a transportation clause (see Chapter 8) insure it for the full amount. Remember the returned article does not belong to the dealer until it is back in his hands. You will, of course, pay the return postage or express.

Here are some other rules for buyers which will make mail-order buying efficient and promote good feeling between buyer and seller:

Don't expect to have a purchase sent C.O.D. Most dealers put this in their ads requesting check or money order with the order.

Don't query a dealer uselessly for things he may not carry. Many dealers advertise their specialties, so read the ads carefully. A self-addressed card with the items on it that you are looking for will make it easy for the dealer to check "yes" or "no" and expedite matters all around.

Send enough postage. Dealers will return excess postage if it is worth doing so or give you credit on your next order. Again a self-addressed envelope will bring back the excess postage more quickly. Express packages can be sent collect.

When returning an article, write a courteous letter saying why you are doing so, or if you have a complaint to make use the soft approach. You may not feel like it when the "slight flake on rim" turns out to be a good-sized chip or a stopper doesn't match. But courtesy pays every time on both sides of the fence. There may be a few dealers who deliberately misrepresent pieces in their ads, but not many. The magazines try to see to this. They don't want this kind of advertising business any more than you do. So if you have been a victim of real misrepresentation notify the magazine.

Be specific about shipping instructions. The dealer may not know that you live nowhere near an express office and that postage, though higher, might work out better for you.

Don't buy emotionally. Be sure of yourself. Buying mail order is no time to change your mind. An ad might be most alluring, but don't respond unless you feel sure you will keep what you order—provided, of course, that it is all that the ad specifies.

There are don'ts for dealers, too. A mail-order customer has a right to demand *reasonable promptness* in filling his order or answering his letter. This is the way the dealer has chosen to do business and he should be equipped to handle it. There is no excuse for carelessness or delays.

Checks, if not used, should be returned promptly. If there is a chance that the article sold to another customer might come back or that a similar article could be substituted, the dealer should notify the sender of the check and ask what he should do about it.

He should also return that excess postage promptly.

He should see that articles are packed properly and carry insurance to cover them in transit.

He should send an invoice with each shipment. There is something then to show if there is a claim for damage or loss.

He should stand back of his ad. Things should be what he says they are, proof if he claims them to be, authentic if he makes that statement as many do. If he advertises "No reproductions" or "Guaranteed old" he should be willing to make good on his mistakes, because everyone can make them. It is very easy to go wrong in identifying a piece or to overlook some slight imperfection. I remember I once bought a pair of lovely apple-green perfume bottles from a dealer I knew who had given me a good price on them. They were supposed to be proof. But when I unpacked them I found one small tip of a scallop was broken off. It could have been overlooked very easily because of the pattern. I didn't know what to do. I felt sure the dealer had no intention of cheating me, yet that broken tip made quite a difference in the value. At last I told him, and received the answer I expected, "Send them back at once, and I'll return your check." But I wanted those bottles. So I decided to keep them, chip and all, and when his check came to make good the depreciation I got just as generous and tore it up. After all, what was a little chip between friends?

Prices should be definitely stated if not in the ad at least on a list or in a letter. And here we come to that much-discussed subject of pricing or not pricing antiques on the tags. There are arguments on both sides. A survey by a magazine that took up this topic showed that 90 per cent of buyers want their antiques marked in dollars and cents, not by code numbers or priced verbally. Many refuse to go into shops that do not price their wares. They are suspicious that it can mean but one thing, the price is made to fit the customer. Others say that the price is a big factor in deciding whether to buy or not, and they like to know what it is before they come to a decision. Certainly it is not pleasant to go through a shop and to have to ask about each piece that interests you, "How much is it?" It gets monotonous and embarrassing when you put it down and pass on. Maybe the dealer is calling you a looker or a nuisance. But if his stock had been priced, you could have sized it up very soon as beyond your budget and walked out, saving his time and your temper.

Some dealers may do this because they are ready to bargain, and you may come out all right in the end. But it does give you a feeling of security to go into a shop, like a favorite one I know, where the dealer says that her prices, clearly marked, are the same for everyone. She gives no discounts but she does keep her prices reasonably low for a quick turnover. It's a pleasure to do business with her.

Reputable dealers asked why they do not price their goods have several explanations for it. They work from the cost which is the code number on the ticket. They say that the interested customer will ask the price, the curiosity seeker doesn't care, and in this way they weed out the serious from the casual. Perhaps.

They point out that with so many dealers buying from each other a published price is not practical. Their wholesale or dealer discount varies too much. For good customers they will do better than for strangers. They also will tell you that they protect themselves in this way from comparative shoppers and undercutting of competitors. This is especially true at sales where it is easy to go from booth to booth comparing prices.

Often a dealer does not know what he ought to charge for an unfamiliar piece. He leaves it unmarked and waits for someone to tip him off on its value.

This pricing or lack of pricing goes on in the mail-order business as well as in the shop. In many ads you will find no prices at all. The dealers say that many articles need more description to explain the price than can be given in a line or two of advertising. If the reader is really interested, he will write. On the other hand, mail-order buyers do not like this either. They say it saves time and letter writing to have the price stated after each article.

Some dealers do not try to list their wares, only their specialties. If you are looking for one thing, you write to those who advertise it. They will send you a list of their pieces. Sometimes they charge for these, 10 cents, 25 cents, or even 50 cents a list, which may be refunded with the first purchase. Sometimes they will send photos of pieces that you pay for also. This saves a lot of querying and writing back and forth. There are other dealers who have a big enough mail-order clientele to warrant their getting out monthly or bimonthly catalogues to send to those on their mailing lists. This is a very handy way to shop for those whose wants fall into the more familiar categories such as pattern glass, china, dolls, bottles, etc.

In shopping by mail there is no reason why you should not do what you do with a shop dealer, register your wants with several dealers and make it easy for them by sending along stamped and self-addressed envelopes for reply. Some dealers even invite you to "write wants."

There is one last resort for the collector, the swap column.

It is not too reliable a way to spot things because often the swapper is not professional and may not give a true description of what he has. It is, however, a way not to be overlooked, especially if the exchange is for the convenience of other specialists like yourself. The trouble is who is to say what the comparative values of the pieces to be swapped are. However, if you are a good horse trader and like the excitement of bargaining, you may come off all right. Here are some typical ads from magazines such as *Hobbies* and *Yankee:*

BITTERS BOTTLES. Swap for other bitters or old medicine bottles.

RURAL SCOUT, PICKER, will trade antiques for coins, guns, jewelry. Send list of your wants. My list for stamped envelope.

I collect American military insignia, shoulder insignia, distinctives (known as regimentals), collar insignia, chevrons, etc. Have coins (none rare) from about 90 different countries. Wanna swop?

Have the old-fashioned "Penny" china dolls. Painted hair and features. Arms and legs wired on. Over 50 years old. Want old cards such as trains, flowers, Indians, state map cards also. Want crochet cotton No. 30 for quilt pieces or what?

In making swaps by way of such ads it is more than likely that some money will have to pass hands, too. But this is all right if you find what you want. You should know your values, however, and be prepared for some correspondence.

5.

WHEN TO COLLECT

WHEN is the best time of life to start collecting? There is no age limit, but there are certain times when it would seem to be a particularly good hobby to pursue. These are in youth and old age. If you begin young, you have several advantages. You get a good start while you have time to devote to it, you acquire the habit and know-how before life gets too demanding, and the things you acquire should be worth much more than you paid for them in your own lifetime. In fact, some parents have gone so far as to start collections for and with their children as nest eggs for college or marriage, or to start them in business. Except for life insurance it is as good a way as any to provide for their future—providing you buy the right things (see Chapter 9).

In the middle years collecting has the same place as any other hobby or pastime. It's a diversion that pays off often in cash as well as in the good health that comes from outside interests and relaxation. Unfortunately, the middle years are the busiest and require the most money for daily living. The father of a family whose education is still ahead of him will not feel he should spend money for something that is going to make a dent in the budget. Moreover, he is usually too busy to give a collection the proper thought. The mother and homemaker will feel the same way, particularly if her spending money must come out of the house pocketbook. Of course this is not a rule. Everyone in the middle years is not so situated. Many young middle-aged couples find great pleasure in collecting together, as witness the husband-and-wife chapters in organizations and clubs of antique enthusiasts.

But for the later years, the years of retirement, collecting is an ideal thing to cultivate. It takes little physical effort. You can antique in a wheel chair if you have to or with a four-cent stamp. These are the years when time is not at a premium. Presuming that your life work has been rewarding, there should be some funds that you can spend without feeling that the money is being taken from others. Dependents should be long on their own. But many older people are too concerned with what they are going to leave behind them and often they turn penurious in order to build up an estate for their dear ones. In this day and age nothing could be more foolhardy. Who knows what the tax situation will be ten years, even five years, from now, or what the dollar that you are putting away now will be worth when you're gone? Young people don't expect inheritances any more. They have become used to the idea that waiting to step into dead men's shoes is a waste of time.

Perhaps the best reason for collecting in your later years is the way this interest sparks your life, keeps the years from showing. You are never too old to tackle something new. An active, alert brain is never too old to learn. So, even if you have reached the Social Security age, don't give up. Look around you for something you can collect and in that way build up your estate, even if you don't live to realize on your investment yourself. An older man who has a small income, which with his Social Security is enough for his wants, deliberately took a small part-time job to keep him busy and give him some interest. As he intended to use the extra money in collecting old guns to add to the few he had picked up over the years, he sought a job with an antique dealer who specialized in guns, doing various handy-man jobs. He didn't make much, he couldn't under Social Security, but he had time to read up on his subject and soon found himself something of an expert as well as the owner of some nice guns, as good as bonds in his safety-deposit box. Moreover, he had a good time doing it.

But what about the young people? Can you get children, particularly the teen-agers, interested in collecting old things? As was pointed out in Chapter 1, if the child has that inborn desire to collect you will have no trouble. You won't be able to stop him but you may be able to direct him. He may outgrow early collections, but as his tastes change he will come back to something else. These are the years when his interest can be fanned by a parent as in the case of the father who took over his young son's stamp book when the boy tired of it and eventually lured his son back to more advanced collecting.

If a child lives in the atmosphere of collecting in a home where others are doing it, he will want to do it, too. It is much like reading. The child who grows up in a home where everyone reads, where books line the walls and are taken as seriously as the food on the table, is pretty sure to turn into a reader himself. It will be the same with collecting.

But what about the older children, the teen-agers whose "will is the wind's will," who turn to this and that and stick at nothing very long? They are very apt to dismiss antiques as "junk" unless, of course, they were indoctrinated quite young or have been tactfully steered into collecting old things that tie in with their current interests. It may take the oblique approach as do so many things in these difficult years. Their lives are already full of the things of the moment, school, sports, music, etc. But most boys and girls have other hobbies or leanings and these can be harnessed to advantage. A typical story is that of a mother who was about to do over her daughter's room. Because she wanted to use old pieces in the décor she took the girl shopping in the antique shops. They started with the desk about which the girl had decided ideas. The mother let the girl do the picking, and when she found a capacious one with a secret drawer, that was it. Then because an old desk required old fittings the mother added a china inkwell in which the girl could keep a quill pen, one that would really write. "I think she saw herself as a Jane Austen or a Louisa May Alcott," her mother tells the story with a laugh. Her father gave her an old seal and sealing wax, and her aunt a glass paperweight with the word *Friendship* in it. Now she is off on her hobby. Everything is *the desk.* Other old pieces were accepted. She no longer calls them old-fashioned. Now when she goes along with her mother on antiquing expeditions she is already keeping her eyes open for more inkwells.

This sort of thing happens over and over in homes where collecting is considered an important pastime. A little fellow who almost from the cradle has shown an inordinate interest in boats will probably turn into a collector of nautical items. Right now his bathtub navy makes his bath a problem. Boats are his picture-book favorites. His parents say he must be a throwback to some seafaring ancestor. Already he has been the guest on ocean-going liners and full-day excursions on

New York tugboats. His father and mother are giving serious thought to steering this interest into a collecting channel. The first thing on the list will be a ship in a bottle, that mysterious thing so sure to fascinate a small boy. Ship models will follow when he is older. He'll probably become a Sea Scout and when he is at the problem age his collection may have enough of a hold to keep him out of mischief.

Collecting cannot, of course, be recommended as a surefire remedy for delinquency. But it can help, taking its place among all the other devices thought up by parents, teachers, and psychologists as deterrents to mischief, vandalism, and worse. Everyone seems to agree that it is the excitement of lawbreaking that turns a good boy or girl into a bad boy or girl, and that it must be fought by supplying equally exciting things that are harmless. Competitive athletics help, so do other organized activities such as clubs, scouting, supervised hot-rod racing, and target practice. Making the adolescents part of some community activity, such as being volunteer firemen or ambulance attendants, has been successful in many places. It is possible to make collecting such a hobby. In many cases it will have no attraction, but it is worth a try. It will require much tact, patience, time, and money.

There was a small-town boy some years ago who was bored because, as he said, "Nothing ever happens here." He was on the edge of a crowd that seemed determined to make things happen, the wrong things, when one day a visiting uncle from the West left behind him a pile of timetables. His interest was caught by the old place names. He got out a map to trace the line of the trip. That was the beginning of an absorbing hobby, collecting timetables and correlating the various lines until he had an elaborate network of the whole railroad picture across the country. He haunted travel agencies and railroad information booths. He hunted out old and extinct lines. By the time he was ready for college he had a really professional accumulation of maps, files, data, etc. Eventually he was able to sell it off to another collector.

There is another interesting story that begins with a boy's interest. This time it was a boy of sixteen who on a trip into the country with his parents discovered an unusual latch on a barn door. He persuaded the farmer to take it off and sell it to him. He was so intrigued with its primitive design and workings that he kept looking for others. Soon he was collecting old hardware right and left. His eagle eye never missed an old hinge or lock or latch. Not a student in the sense of the word that would send him to college, he began to dig into the history of iron in this country. He made trips to England and brought back fine old locks, keys, etc. Today, not much more than ten years later, he is one of the foremost authorities on early American iron hardware in the country and besides selling it for restoration purposes has a fine collection of his own.

In reading the stories of famous collections you will find that they often began in childhood. In Alec Templeton's book about his music boxes he tells that it really began when he heard his first one in Wales as a child. In Aline B. Saarinen's book, *The Proud Possessors,* she tells the story of Electra Havemeyer Webb who started as a child collecting turtles, and ended up with 125,000 objects of early American arts and crafts. One big wholesale dealer in antiques keeps intact the big cabinet of miniature Pennsylvania Dutch pieces which she started to collect as a little girl.

Naturally some things more than others will appeal to the young collector. For the little girl there are, of course, dolls. As a starter it might be well not to limit her too narrowly to antique dolls. Let her grow into that as her knowledge of old dolls increases. Gradually she will pass by the modern foreign, costume, character, and storybook dolls for more important things such as china heads, Greiners, etc.

Everybody knows how a child adores a button box. It will keep the pre-school child busy for hours sorting out and stringing the buttons. So why not start the little girl with an old button string to which she can add? The first buttons do not have to be valuable only storied, but soon some will ap-peal more than others and before you know it you will have a confirmed button collector in the family. Even boys will like collecting military buttons.

A button collector recently pointed out to me that buttons are an ideal collectible for children. Except for rare ones they are cheap, and as almost everyone has an old button box, contributions are sure to pour in. She showed me some but-ton cards that would delight any child. They are similar to the "projects" that youngsters do for school with buttons attached with pipe cleaners or invisible wire hairpins to backgrounds that relate to the button classification. These backgrounds may be painted or drawn in, pasted on, or done in needlework. Thus for a circus picture she had assembled a number of large spherical buttons in various colors and materials at the ends of painted-on cords for balloons under a big top of pasted-on red-and-white-striped paper. There were other paste-ons of circus figures, and looking fierce be-tween the bars of a painted cage was a large lion button. Any child could do this. Shoe buttons which are old and of great variety can be sewn to felt cutouts in the shape of high-button shoes. Flower buttons can bloom on embroidered stems from an appliquéd pot. Another idea that will appeal to a young person is to illustrate the record of a vacation trip with buttons sewn into the typed or written text in place of a word much like a rebus, such as "We saw a [flock of geese button] and a place that looked like [a castle—button]."

School children will like to make button "projects" by mounting their buttons on cards, assembling those of a similar nature, and adding cutouts or drawings or even embroidery to carry out the motif. For instance, they will love to make a Christmas tree using colored glass and round metal buttons for balls and trimming, or a bouquet with gay buttons blooming on painted or embroidered stems, or a seashore scene with shell buttons or those showing marine life. It will give zest and reason to their collecting.

Never throw perfume bottles away if there is a girl in the family. Let her treasure them on a shelf in her own room. She may want to fill them with colored water and put them on a window shelf. What she collects today may seem valueless, but ten years from now the Schiaparelli-waisted woman and the Matchabelli crown may be worth good, hard cash just as the old bottles of yesterday are bringing in the dollars now. As she progresses, she will be the first to spot the older perfume bottles in shops and at sales.

Another bottle field for the young collector is the figural bottle and its cousin, the candy container. These appeal to a child's sense of humor. They are funny. They still do not cost so much that they will be a strain on the allowance or Dad's pocketbook. In the same class are what antique collectors call grotesqueries, queer faces, heads and figures in china, glass, metal, etc., things such as the satyr masks, unusual Tobies, devils, and jack o' lanterns. In line with these are the whimseys, the hats, shoes, hatchets, gypsy kettles, canoes, etc., in glass and china. Also to be classed with these more or less humorous novelties are the banks. Most mechanical banks are too high priced for the young collector but there are many others in glass, wood, pottery, as well as iron, animals, books, buildings, figures, etc., that will make good teen-age conversation pieces. A young person may even get interested in what can be called the What's Its or Gimmicks whose origin and use are a mystery.

No boy or girl will have to be persuaded to save postcards. Today, with the interest in old cards mounting among collectors, they should prove a fine introduction into the field for young people.

For a young girl things that pertain to the toilet or vanity table should be surefire—jewel boxes, trinket boxes, photo frames, fans, mirrors, old jewelry, such as bangles for her old link bracelet, beads, romantic lockets, perhaps pincushions or even miniature lamps. For her room she may go in for flower or fashion prints. If she likes to sew, she may collect thimbles, samplers, needlecases, and sewing birds. If she likes to do craft work, she may get interested in old scissors pictures or decoupage. If she is musical, old sheet music ought to open up a wide collecting field. If she is religiously inclined, there are Bible pictures, madonnas, angels, medals, or pictures of her patron saint.

Figurines fascinate children—cherubs, dancers, romantic shepherds and shepherdesses, Red Ridinghood, and other storybook characters. Valentines belong to the young. It is not too soon to collect them even before you begin to think of love. Spoons interest many girls, especially souvenir spoons, as do quaint napkin rings. One of the favorite collectibles of all ages is bells. They are not to be by-passed if you are trying to get your child interested in collecting antiques. Their sound as much as their function will be enough to start a little girl on the chase. Boys like them, too, but will go in for different kinds. Long after they have stopped believing in Santa Claus their love for the mythical old saint may start a collection, or they may cherish the china and blown decorated Easter eggs left over from Easter Bunny days.

What is there about boxes that is so intriguing? Children feel it, too. Pandora set the fashion in making boxes mysterious. There are all kinds of old and interesting boxes for the young collector which do not necessarily cost much to own.

A favorite basis for collecting among young girls is to gather up anything that bears her first name. If she has a fairly common one, she is in luck. Imagine, however, the joy of a young girl who came upon a bonnet stand at an antique show bearing her name, Claire. Favorite flowers motivate many a young girl's collecting—roses, violets, etc., as do hearts.

An accident will often start the young collector on his way. Take the teen-ager who was giving an outdoor party at a summer camp where there was no electricity, but rummaging in an old chest she found a pile of Japanese paper lanterns. They so fascinated her that she decided to look for more. Or the little girl who came upon a box of glass prisms from an old chandelier and strung them up for a wind bell. When someone explained that they were real antiques she looked at them a bit differently and added to them to string across her window in a festoon of dancing lights. Or the girl who went in for mugs because she saw her first collection at a kitchen raid in a friend's house.

All children like small things, not only dollhouse furnishings but other small collectibles such as miniature books, small-scale reproductions, and salesman's samples, or in the case of boys models of things such as locomotives, autos, etc.

Collecting animal figures is of course a natural beginning

for the young collector. The girl who likes cats is remembered by all her friends when a gift or a souvenir is in order. The same thing holds for the boy who goes in for horses or dogs. Cows, lambs, birds, chickens, roosters, pigs, elephants, even mice and fish from the ranks of antiques will find their way to a young collector's heart. Here again it might be wise not to try to limit them, at least at first, to the old. They will become more discriminating with time.

Let's see what little boys' collections are made of besides frogs and snails and puppy dogs' tails. Boys love guns. Dad will have to hold the hand here but not for long. He'll be giving Dad pointers on age, makers, etc., in no time. Powder flasks and horns are just as fascinating and less dangerous. After guns come knives, which offer enough from swords to bowie knives to keep a young fellow busy and off the street. Horns and whistles will figure importantly for some boys. If he's a jazz enthusiast, he'll perhaps collect drums, and of course the early jazz records. If he is the outdoor type, he may go along with Dad and specialize in decoys or in traps and snares. If a horse lover, he'll look for horse brasses, bridle rosettes, horse prints, spurs, old currycombs, etc.

As far as old toys go it will be the early train sets that will interest him most, possibly marbles or puppets. If he is mechanical, he may want to tinker with old clocks or locks. A summer on a farm may inspire him to pick up old farm implements or tools at country sales. Other interests will spur collections such as circus or Wild West posters, sleight-of-hand material, old cameras, skates, handcuffs, license plates, military hats and caps, chessmen, baseballs, and even early electric bulbs. If he is a hero worshiper of some historic personage he'll find much to inspire a collection.

How are you going to finance the young collector? Unless

he chooses something quite low in price it can't be done out of the regular allowance. On the other hand, it is not good policy for Dad or Mother to put his or her hand in the pocket every time something new for the collection comes up. Probably the best way is to put the young collector on a budget for his hobby, either with an account he may draw on himself or against one doled out by the parents. It isn't likely that a young person is going to go on buying sprees very often. But it will teach him to compare and evaluate before he steps in to buy if his finances are limited. Many of his collectibles are going to be given him for birthday and Christmas gifts, or doting relatives will give him checks to buy his own.

It will be up to the parent to decide the speed with which the young person adds to his collection, often enough to sustain interest, seldom enough to make him discriminating. If the teen-age collection can coincide in some way with the parents' own interests in antiques it will be easier to keep an eye on it. It will be just one more way to keep the family together—and for that reason alone is worth all the work and money it may entail.

6.

WHY COLLECT?

ASIDE from the compulsion that drives the natural collector to accumulate his treasures, the therapeutic value of collecting as a release from tension, or the investment element that might motivate the canny collector, there are other reasons or at least by-products that might be called the intangibles which answer the question, "Why do you collect antiques?" There are many people who will ask this question in an amused or patronizing way. With so much going on in the world today, with space taking on definite dimensions, they believe collecting the dead things of the past a silly avocation. The beginning collector may not be able to answer the question because he may not know what makes him tick, why his heart beats a bit faster when he sees a china perfume bottle that *might* be Tucker at the back of a shelf.

The lure of antiques is hard to analyze. It stems from so many things, probably the strongest being a desire to be a knowledgeable part of a heritage that is beginning to take on age and dignity. Now we can say, "This piece goes back two hundred years," or even "two hundred and fifty years," and we begin to hold up our heads among the older nations. We also find that in gathering up our antiques that our society

65

when new was not such a rough, primitive affair as has been pictured. Certainly our antiques, as well as showing the ingenuity of our primitive arts and crafts, also showed pictures of gracious living, even luxurious living, that could hold its own today by many modern standards. We look at an early silver tea service or a Philadelphia highboy, or a beautiful amethyst glass hall lantern, and we say, "They certainly knew how to live in those days."

There is also the factor of craftsmanship to attract the lover of the old. In this day of mass production the handmade piece is rare. We like to gather around us the things that men who loved their crafts fashioned slowly and painstakingly, each piece a personal accomplishment. In fact, it is the end of hand craftsmanship and the beginning of the machine age that the government has considered in setting the date of 1830 as defining antiques.

Among many collectors there is a feeling of responsibility. Someone should be cherishing these relics of the past before they are destroyed or lost. If it weren't for the farseeing collectors of the turn of the century or earlier we might not have today the assemblage of early blown glass, Pilgrim furniture, Philadelphia silver, New England pewter, and so on. Every collector of antiques today, no matter how seemingly unimportant the thing he collects, does this same thing in a small way. Every advanced collector who goes in for researching in the murky archives of the past for the origins, names of makers, dates, places of manufacture, etc., adds something to the history of production in this country or to the saga of American mores covering more than three hundred years.

All these things, pride in our heritage and the growth of our country, admiration for the crafts which a young, untrained nation produced, the urge to go on filling in the picture, are some of the intangibles that come to every collector of antiques who is at all serious. There are others. There is a feeling of accomplishment, a sense of triumph, when a hard-to-find piece is unearthed, both very good for the ego. For the shy person, for someone who finds it hard to express himself in other ways, who feels lacks he cannot fill perhaps in education, skills, etc., the mere collecting of good things will give him confidence. The minute he finds out that he knows more about a certain thing than others may, he takes on stature and gains some faith in himself. It spurs him on to new accomplishments in many fields.

There is no doubt that collecting can enrich your life. No matter how humdrum the daily grind, how uninteresting the breadwinning vocation, if there is this exciting business of collecting to turn to, you are not lost in the slough of mediocrity. It not only brings interest into your daily living but it makes you a more interesting person on your own. You have something to talk about besides recipes, clothes, taxes, and labor problems.

One of the most important of the intangibles is that in collecting you "meet the nicest people." It enlarges your scope in making friends. The quiet little man in your office to whom you merely nod or say "Good morning" may prove to have one of the finest collections of old watches in town. Or the librarian who stamps your books without looking at you will suddenly open up when she finds you taking out a book on lacy glass which she, too, collects. You may not be the "joiner" type. Clubs and associations may have no appeal for you. But when you collect and in some way find yourself with a group of fellow collectors who can talk shop, you forget all about this anti-social instinct and look forward to club meetings with a zest.

Somewhere in the preceding chapters I made the statement that the person who collects is usually a pretty nice person to have around. He is never bored. He is not self-centered, because his interests have been directed outward. He is not apt to become a victim of compulsory vices that take money. His only vice is collecting, if you want to call it a vice, for of course it can be, as can anything that is done to extremes or siphons off money that should be used in other ways. But that is something that can be controlled. Done intelligently and with a sense of adventure, collecting can be one of the most exciting and satisfying of hobbies.

Good luck to you!

7.

HOW TO DISPLAY
YOUR COLLECTION

I BELIEVE a collection to be thoroughly enjoyed should be put on view not occasionally but every day. It should be an integral part of the furnishings of the home. Some people may not agree with me. They may feel that simple accomplishment is enough, that it fills its purpose even though hidden away in a closet or drawers or even in cartons in the attic or garage. Now there may be some things valuable as collectibles that you would not care to display, but even these unattractive things can be kept properly in places that are more suitable for them. A playroom or large family room can have its corners turned over to such things as cigar-store Indians or its walls filled with weather vanes and old signs. Guns on racks or pegs can line the wall of a man's study or a boy's room or even an entrance hall if you do not want them in the living room. Canes can be treated the same way. Farm implements can be hung in a small shed devoted just to them, or even on the walls of a garden room. Or lacking that, they can be featured on one wall of the garage. At least they are on view.

A garden room, incidentally, offers an opportunity for

displaying many things you would not want in the house. One collector who goes in for crockery jars finds the place for them on a sheltered terrace.

But generally speaking, most collections have a decorative value if they are used the right way. In fact, ingenuity in displaying them is part of the fun. The most obvious way, of course, for all kinds of china, glass, silver, or other small objects is to show them off in cabinets and open cupboards. Special built-in cupboards are fine if you have the room and the kind of house that will take them. In one home where the various collections might take over if left to themselves several wall cabinets have been built with a small-paned glass door and angled side panels of glass like small bay windows, the wood painted to match the other woodwork in each room. They are not too conspicuous even in an upper hall and bedroom.

But it adds to the picture and the décor generally if you use other antiques to show off your collections, hanging wall cupboards, corner cupboards with or without doors (a good chance to use part of an old cupboard that may have lost its base or doors), bookcases, secretaries, breakfronts, and whatnots. Even old china closets of the Victorian era can be modernized by removing the legs, gimcracks, etc.

Now while it makes for order to keep a collection together in one place I have seen them scattered over a house in such a way that you were scarcely conscious of them as a collection. I have in mind a collection of apothecary jars, rather overwhelming if kept in one place. But they were distributed on mantelpieces, side tables, window sills, the piano, even on upstairs dressing tables and highboys as so many pieces of decorative vases or bric-a-brac. Often they were used for flowers. Until you were aware of them or had them pointed out to you, you had no idea that the owner, a druggist by the way, had a really outstanding collection in his home.

Another young man I know who has gone in almost professionally for stoneware, crocks, jars, jugs, etc., lives in a small suburban house where they could prove a problem. But he solves it ingeniously by placing his larger pieces on his stairs, one to each step close to the wall. Smaller pieces are used throughout the house like the apothecary jars. Others are used outside on his terrace. Though the collection is sizable, it never takes over the house yet is immediately available for interested guests to examine.

On the other hand, I know of another small house where the whole downstairs overflows with one woman's collecting done over the years. One is afraid to move through the rooms cluttered with tables full of milk glass, majolica, teapots, taffeta glass, slag, and pattern-glass pieces. Every piece of furniture except the chairs carries a load, even in the breakfast room. You wonder where the family eats, how they entertain. The clutter is so overwhelming that you lose sight of the fact that there are many fine and important things about. Here is an example of the "point of saturation" which many collectors reach. Once started, it is hard to stop. Maybe it is time for her to begin to sell off.

I am reminded also of another house, a small one in a small town, where the owners had gone in for majolica in a big way. What they had collected was significant. They had done their best to contain it in their dining room with closets and shelves but it was overflowing into the living room, too, taking over the house, turning it from a home into a museum. I was not surprised to hear that they have moved, built themselves a new home out of town with one large room lined with cabinets just to take care of their collection.

Many collectors find it advantageous to give up a room to their collection. There is the man who collects iron toys and banks. He has taken the garage attached to the house and made it into a room for his collectibles. The car now stands in a carport. A woman whose hobby is pitchers uses her sun porch to display them among her plants. At the windows she uses iron plant and lamp brackets to hold some of her finest pitchers, anchoring them well with small rubber mats. Some of her pitchers are used as planters for trailing ivy and vines. Across the top of the window is a frieze of pitchers on hooks, safer, she says, than a shelf. In two corners of the room are wire plant stands where more pitchers parade between pots of flowering plants. Glass pitchers fill the shelves against the windows that stay stationary. The whole thing is quite charming.

While it might prove an expensive project for a home, I can't help mentioning here a clever way of using glass plates seen in a well-known Maryland restaurant. The owner had gone in for square plates and had had them incorporated into a large window, a plate to a pane. The effect was most breathtaking.

Lighting is an important feature when planning a display of your collectibles. It is foolish to hide them in the dark recesses of a cupboard. If you have an important piece, don't be afraid to spotlight it from a hidden source. Any closet or cupboard can be lighted with a row of small bulbs or fluorescent tubes placed behind the sides or top of the frame where they won't show. Recently in a cabinetmaker's shop I saw a fine walnut bookcase made as a companion piece to match an old one in the home of a woman who collects fine glass. The clever maker had wired it with invisible lighting bulbs under each shelf with a button and switch on the outside at one end and an inconspicuous cord ready to be plugged into a base socket. Often using colored bulbs will give glamor and throw a kinder light on some things.

Many pieces can be seen to advantage and removed from the areas of use by using shelves placed in unused doorways, windows, or closets, or on room dividers. By opening up a closet or doorway between rooms you have the advantage of light from both sides and an illusion of space. If the door or closet cannot be opened at the back, it can be filled in with glass brick to admit daylight or artificial light. Of course glass shelves are an ideal way to display glass, especially colored glass. Even old bottles with little artistic appeal will take on a glamour on a window shelf where light can shine through them. Naturally you don't want shelves on a window with a view, but where you want privacy they are almost as good as a shade. On a picture window that really frames a vista it is possible to use one shelf across the top for interest and color. Sometimes an odd window needed for light but otherwise an eyesore can be treated like one I know in the passage between two parts of an old house. All along the sides and over the top were jars of trailing vines to hide the unattractive woodwork and on the glass shelves was a collection of gay red-and-white souvenir glass pieces. It was an asset rather than a liability.

Another way to save space when housing collections is to hang them on the wall wherever possible. Wall treatments can be fashioned from shadow boxes and old clock cases to hold small pieces. Wooden panels can be cut out on which to mount butter pats or cup plates or dish lids. Other flat things, such as plates, trivets, miniatures, silhouettes, horse brasses, fire marks, cookie cutters, tiles, daguerreotype cases, etc., can be arranged symmetrically in groups over furniture or used as borders around doorways, windows, fireplaces, etc. A shelf close to the ceiling around several walls of the room is a fine way to get the collectibles out of the way without clutter, but they should not be too high to see or to handle without a stepladder.

Antiques for displaying antiques can make for interesting décor. If your treasures must be kept under glass, shop for some old vitrines, those small cases used for displays in shops, or even plain, old-fashioned counter cases. One of these on a table under some shelves will not look out of place if it is painted to match and lined with interesting paper or material. Old spool cabinets make wonderful repositories for spoons, jewelry, or even prints. Unframed prints can be kept in portfolios in a Canterbury or music cabinet. A pierced-tin pie cupboard usually has shelves deep enough to take files of old magazines, scrapbooks, etc. Get or have copied an old spoon rack or a pair of them for displaying your finest spoons. An ox yoke in the kitchen or over an old fireplace makes a fine piece on which to hang iron kitchen or hearth pieces. The pegs of an old accordion hatrack will take care of a primitive collection that can be hung up, powder horns, shaving mugs, lanterns, etc. All the many-drawered cabinets from old drugstores, doctors' or dentists' offices, architects' offices, machine shops, old grocery stores, as well as spice cabinets, make fine filing cases for small collectibles. Remember the old revolving bookcase, square or round? Its shelves are suited for displaying a collection if it can stand the motion of being rotated, old banks, for instance. Large gilt frames are ideal for making the top of glass-topped tables for displaying small curios. Simply hinge them to the side of a shallow box which has been mounted on a pedestal or legs. Use a fine old stone crock in which to house your canes or umbrellas or parasols. No matter if the material is gone, if the handle is good just keep it and the ferrule. One collector of old handles turned an old chest of shallow drawers into a cabinet for her pieces, displaying them on velvet trays that could be lifted out.

Sometimes it is wiser to display only part of a collection at a time. It saves confusion and pieces can be changed or brought out at will. Or only the best can be featured and the less interesting kept under cover. Thus a collector of valentines has picked out her best and finest for framing, leaving the rest in glassine envelopes in cardboard filing boxes which have been covered with decorative paper and kept on her bookshelves for ready reference.

What to do with those yellow pottery pudding molds might stump some women but not the possessor of a collection of about thirty of them. Across the top of her huge shelf above a kitchen fireplace in a very old house she used a second shelf painted white like the plaster. The molds, yellow and white, parade on their sides, bottoms out, across the two shelves and make a most interesting bit of décor in her old kitchen.

An interesting way to display a collection is a tree. A woman who collects the blown decorated Easter eggs has made a permanent egg tree for her hall table by using a real tree branch trimmed to shape, painted green and shellacked, and planted in a fine old jardiniere filled with pebbles. Stylized trees made from wooden branches have been used for collections of things such as sewing birds, bells, or thimbles.

Another novel arrangement which could be adapted for many things was made from two long strips of wide velvet ribbon in a heavenly blue. On them was a collection of Madonna prints cut from Christmas cards and each one framed in, believe it or not, the brassy metal rings of preserve jar lids. Buttons mounted on velvet show off to advantage, as do souvenir spoons.

Lithophanes have no interest until there is a light behind them. While many can be found as used originally in candle screens, lampshades, and other items, many more picked up by the collector are unframed or unmounted plaques. For these a collector I know has found several interesting uses. He has set a series of portrait lithophanes into the wooden doors of built-in corner cupboards in his living room with lights concealed inside the cupboards to show up the pictures. In every spot where he needs a ceiling light he uses a lithophane to mask the recessed bulb rather than plain glass. They are even set into lighted panels over doorways and thus become decorative wall pieces instead of a collection of white lifeless glass plates.

Another decorative wall has been designed by the collector of horse bridle rosettes which for a time he kept in shallow pans of sand. But when a new house was built and a small study off the living room designed for his trophies and horse prints, he put in a whole wall of wallboard back of a davenport. He had it cut in slits just large enough to take the shank of a bridle button and close enough together so that the buttons almost touched. By careful selection he turned his button board into a decorative mosaic yet any button can be removed or replaced at a moment's notice.

Maybe other women have thought of making hatpin bouquets even if they do not have the old hatpin holders to keep them in. Any old vase will do if it is filled with sand or pebbles to hold the pins in a flower arrangement.

Old keys are not beautiful to look at but they can become something quite interesting if they are strung on an old wire key ring or one fashioned from heavy wire to be used as door knockers. They can be used outside if they are kept waxed against rust. Shoe lasts make good door knockers if there is any way of attaching a concealed hinge to them. Which brings up an important point in using collectibles that have value. *Never, never make any adaptations that will destroy the original piece or alter it* unless you have no desire to preserve it as an antique or as a part of your collection. Many a good piece has been irrevocably damaged by good-intentioned do-it-yourselfers as far as value is concerned. This is an unbreakable rule wherever antiques are adapted by responsible authorities for modern use. In Winterthur Museum, Wilmington, Delaware, where the effect of candlelight is important, all fixtures are wired without breaking into them in any way. Where wires cannot be threaded through brackets, they are made almost invisible by selecting thin wiring of the same color and tying it on at intervals with colored thread.

There is a difference of opinion about using antiques from a collection for everyday purposes. I can't see why not if they are not harmed by it. A set of old tiles set into a fireplace or table top or window sill is far more interesting than the same tiles piled away in a corner. Why not use glass or china pieces for fruit or flowers or plants? Or serve your tea in Chelsea cups? The objection is, of course, the danger of breakage. So it depends upon how you look at it. Personally, I prefer to enjoy a fine piece and take the risk.

There are many ways of using pieces from a collection that will do no harm. Especially is this true of furniture, the small pieces that would look rather silly set in a row merely for display. For instance, if you have a leaning toward stools you can use them in various ways. Everyone knows how handy stools are for television viewing, so that quite a few can be tucked around the living room for that purpose. This holds more for the ottoman or bench than for low footstools. But even those, particularly the very low wooden ones that were designed to keep feet off the cold floors of early American houses, can be used for plant stands or as shelves to hold other collectibles.

Take chests as a collectible. What you find may range all the way from tin document boxes through dolls' trunks, small traveling chests, dowry chests, Bible boxes, and so on. They have innumerable uses that will not destroy their original lines or decorations. There is nothing to prevent lining an old Bible box with jeweler's flannel and having it fitted with a removable tray for holding silver. It can stand on one of the dining-room pieces, or a stand made for it. Chests make fine repositories for paper oddments, prints, maps, etc., or for needlework, or other hobby material. One woman who hooks rugs keeps all her woolen materials in wooden blanket chests, collecting them with an eye to their usefulness as well as beauty. They are easily mothproofed, and no eyesore for hallway, living room, or bedrooms.

How to store old music may offer some problems. The obvious way is to bind it in book form or in large loose-leaf scrapbooks. But the value of some old music lies more in the cover than the score. Here can be found some fine examples of early art printing. One collector has framed a series of covers of old dances, showing colored pictures of couples doing the gavotte, polka, varsovienne, mazurka, etc. This same man has made use of a series of four lovely portrait pictures from the covers of old music of the mid-1800's to decorate the four panels of a square lampshade for a tall lamp.

While it would be desecration to trim an old print of value or to paste it upon something else to display it, there are plenty of interesting prints to be picked up that are not too valuable or costly to be used in various ways. The nicest thing to do with a series of prints is to make them into a screen. You may even be able to do it without harming them if you space them without cutting them on panels of plywood or other material and using rubber cement for holding them in place. You can even paper a small room, a book corner, or a powder room with prints by attaching them to the wallpaper with rubber cement.

If you do decide to use part of your collection for another purpose, try to do so with dignity and with no distortion. There is nothing that so outrages the lover of fine antiques as to see good pieces turned into "cute" accessories, planters, lamps, etc. Sometimes such adaptation turns out well, but often it is nothing but a farce.

Now fine antiques must be protected as well as displayed, and it is not wise to leave them out exposed to dust, dampness, or extremes of heat and cold. Everyone who has owned old furniture has experienced what the change in atmosphere will do to it. It was not made for dry, overheated rooms. It is well to keep heat uniform and moist if you can or at least keep old pieces away from radiators or registers. Never leave water in a fine piece of china or glass. Not only can it be forgotten and left to freeze in a closed unheated house but minerals in the water can cloud the glass. Water left in wood will swell and sometimes crack it, in tin it will rust.

All the careful dusting in the world will not keep a certain dinginess from creeping into certain things such as fans, pincushions, samplers, dolls, wax pieces, carved wood, and so on. They should be kept under or behind glass. Fine fans deserve fine fan frames if you can afford them, if not plain picture frames will do. Saran wrap is a handy way to protect against dust and tarnish, but who wants to see his antiques in shrouds? Bell glasses, old ones or the new ones that can be bought now, are useful for enclosing perishable things such as old watches, figurines, etc. For temporary protection use a plain goblet or brandy glass turned upside down.

The dusting and washing of antiques should never be left to untrained hands. Better face the fact that a collection takes care and that if you do it yourself there will be nobody else to blame for breakage or damage. It can be a chore or a labor of love. In this age of air conditioners and room purifiers dusting is not the problem it once was. A silicon dustcloth will keep down the work. Frequent use of the vacuum cleaner and its attachments keeps the dust away so the collection does not have to be disturbed too often.

Many collectors like to have their metal pieces lacquered to save polishing. It is a help, but eventually they will darken. After all, there is nothing that can compare with the fine patina that shows up with hand rubbing. To keep silver bright, drawers can be lined with the cloth that jewelers use, and in cabinets it helps to keep a lump of camphor with the silver. However, as one silversmith says, just keep your doors closed *tight*. Silver won't tarnish without air.

Perhaps the collections that deteriorate most are those made of paper, ephemera as they are rightly called. How to keep them from yellowing and crumbling with age is a problem. Keeping them pasted in scrapbooks is not too good an idea if you should want to remove them. Photo corners are a better way to hold them, or slip them in glassine envelopes which can be pasted to a page or are part of the scrapbook.

There are times when a spraying with krylon, the colorless liquid plastic in a can, is called for. To preserve old paper boxes with transfer prints or hatboxes covered with wallpaper or even pieces of old wallpaper, a krylon coating will do no harm, but for anything that can be kept under glass, such as old prints, it would be foolish and disastrous. If your prints are valuable enough to frame, see that the framing is done well so that no dust or dampness can get in behind the glass.

And watch the sunshine. While it can do you a good turn and change your old glass into beautiful amethyst shades, it can wreck other things. In fact, sunlight focusing through a glass piece can scorch old paper or fabric.

Moths are no respecters of antiques. If you have anything they can attack, keep it mothproofed. A spraying every few months will do it. And don't forget the silverfish. They will go for so many things, particularly paper. Spray all your boxes, drawers, and bookcases that contain old papers, prints, books, and magazines regularly with a good moth repellent. There is on the market a packaged product supposed to keep silver moths away. Damp closets breed mildew, so keep them dry with a bag of commercial pellets which can be taken out and dried from time to time. There are various soaps and cleaners to keep old leather soft. Linens should be sunned and bleached regularly if you don't want them to yellow or show those brown spots of age. Never attempt to clean an old print or painting yourself unless you have been taught how to do it. If it has any value, it is worth a professional's care.

One thing that is very important in displaying your fine things is to see that they are safe against vibration. A heavy truck moving down a highway can set up enough motion to work a glass shelf from its brackets, send pieces sliding off shelves, loosen up nails or hangers in walls, and so on. Plates set against a wall should always have the protection of a pair of small rubber-headed tacks hammered into the shelf. Or a narrow quarter-round can be nailed along the back of the shelf as a guard. The grooves in old cupboards which once held platters upright are scarcely enough. Either groove them deeper or use the molding or tack method. Cups and pitchers hung on hooks should have the hook pinched tight enough to keep them from slipping off. Be careful, however, that they are not so tight that they will pinch the handle and break it.

To keep glass shelves from working off the ends beyond the metal brackets either drive a small nail into the woodwork as a stopper or use a gummed tape on the metal under the glass. A piece of gummed tape that can be easily removed on the bottom of glass pieces will hold them from sliding off shelves. Baize pasted to the bottom of china or other ornaments saves table tops but it will hide any china markings. Better, use a ring of gummed felt tape instead, or a rubber jar ring.

One of the finest collections of U.S. coin glass in this country has been amassed by Mr. Thomas Schock of Parkesburg, Pa. (*Photo by the Philadelphia Inquirer*)

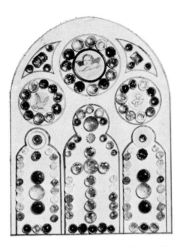
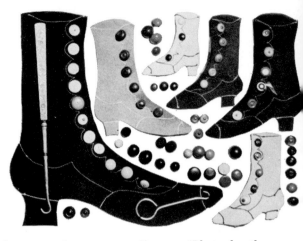

Button projects like these appeal to young collectors. (*Photo by the Philadelphia Inquirer*)

Coronation items from the extensive collection of Mr. Herbert Ward of Lumberville, Pa. (*Photo by the Philadelphia Inquirer*)

This beautiful window made from square glass plates is part of the
décor in Mrs. Kay's Toll House restaurant in Silver Springs, Md.

A part of Mrs. Carson Potter's lavish collection of art-glass vases is displayed in her formal living room. *(Photo by Russell Salmon)*

A thoroughly modernized country kitchen is a fine place to display homespun items. *(Photo by the Philadelphia Inquirer)*

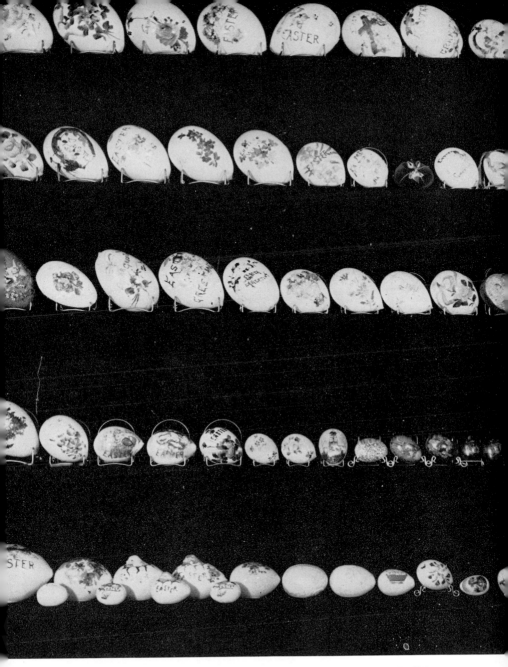

A fine collection of Easter eggs started when a child has sent Judith
Eckel of Johnston, Pa., down the paths of research.

Old Irish Belleck china finds a home in this new cabinet of Mrs. James Brennan of Paoli, Pa. (*Photo by Ned Goode*)

A large collection of milk glass shows to advantage on these built-in shelves surrounding a doorway. (*Photo by Ned Goode*)

A pewter cupboard in the home of Mr. and Mrs. William Jordan of New Castle, Del., is filled with old marked pieces. (*Photo by Ellsworth J. Gentry*)

A small collection of ironstone belonging to the author shows up in an old pine-pie cupboard with pierced tin panels. (*Photo by Russell Salmon*)

The bottle collection from Coventry Forge Inn, Chester County, Pa., is kept in an architecturally important built-in cupboard lighted from the inside. (*Photo by Russell Salmon*)

Glass-labeled apothecary shelf ware preserved in the Stabler-Leadbeater Apothecary Shop, Alexandria, Va., one of the many such restorations throughout the country. (*Courtesy Spinning Wheel*)

Mr. William Roup of Pottstown, Pa., lines the wall of his hobby room with his famous collection of mechanical banks. Other walls hold still other banks and iron toys. (*Photo by William Weiss*)

Surprising variety is the feature of a hatpin-holder collection owned by Mrs. Jacobus deVries of Lakewood, Ohio. (*Courtesy Spinning Wheel*)

The miniature-lamp collection of Mr. Robert Schafer of Stowe, Ohio, shows quality as well as quantity.

Mrs. Paul Sigler of Knightstown, Ind., used this photo of her lamp collection for a Christmas card. (*Courtesy Spinning Wheel*)

The Country Store Museum of the Baldwin Book Barn, West Chester, Pa., began as a private collection fifteen years ago. (*Photo by Tom Hacker*)

Mrs. Bess Bardens of Ambler, Pa., founder and past president of the Questers, takes pride in her famous collection of tea caddies and tea-caddy spoons, of which these silver ones are just a few. (*Photo by Russell Salmon*)

Mrs. Jessie Boyer of Chester County, Pa., was a small girl when she started this collection of primitive carved wooden animals. (*Photo by Russell Salmon*)

Old tools in a modern setting are displayed in the office of an architect, David B. Maxfield of Oxford, Ohio. (*Courtesy Spinning Wheel*)

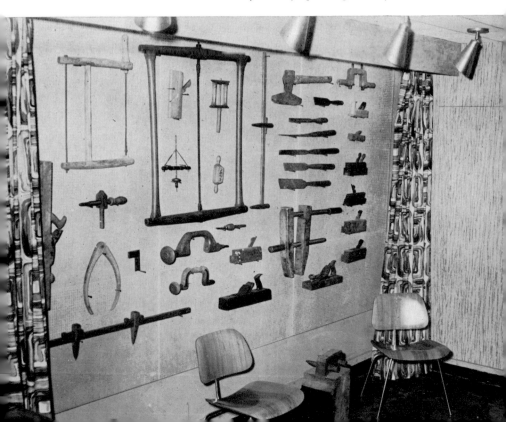

An array of distinctive butter pats from the collection of Mrs. Robert
Lacy of Baltimore, Md. (*Photo by Patton*)

8.

INSURING YOUR COLLECTION

IT IS surprising how many people give no thought to protecting their collection with the proper insurance. Not until a box of old silver spoons disappears mysteriously from a buffet drawer or a cleaning woman knocks over an Imari platter or boys get into the house during your vacation and use a fine primitive portrait for a bull's-eye will you begin to wish you had some kind of insurance policy under which you could make a claim.

Perhaps it is because so many people are not insurance-minded. They are the optimists who will go as far as life or car insurance and perhaps a fire coverage on the home, but that is all. As one otherwise responsible householder recently told an agent who was trying to sell him a liability policy, "This insurance business is all right, I guess, but it can get topheavy. It's like being property poor. It's a luxury. If I took every policy that someone tried to sell me I couldn't afford to live in this property we're talking about right now, nor drive the car I do."

Well, we can leave the argument about that to the insurance salesman. He will have good and cogent answers. And if he is an honest representative of a reliable company he will be the first to admit that too much insurance is a possibility in some cases. There are people who are policy-happy. But insuring a collection of any value certainly makes sense. If you have accumulated something that represents a good outlay of money, something that is fragile, easily pilfered, that can be consumed by fire or damaged by smoke or water and is not easily replaced for what you paid for it, or at all, it seems the wise thing to do to protect yourself. The money you get for a claim that is honored will not get the piece back for you, true, but it will make it possible for you to replace the article if not with the same thing with something else you have been yearning for. From the investment angle you are as well off, you have sustained no loss.

You may feel your collection is well taken care of, properly housed, locked up, perhaps, that very little can happen to it. But things can, the most unexpected things, and not only to the whole collection but to single items in it. For instance, while a home was closed on a business trip, lightning struck and cracked a toilet tank in the bathroom, causing the water to run for days, walls and floors to get soaked, the heater to burn out, and—of interest here—to completely ruin a doll collection on living-room shelves under the bathroom floor and a group of silhouettes on a dripping wall. An explosion of dynamite blasting nearby can loosen a whole glass shelf holding glass pieces and send them crashing. Or sun shining through a glass bottle can scorch or even burn a hole in an old coverlet. An undetected roof leak in an attic can seep into a chest and watermark a collection of old prints. It isn't only fire and theft that are the hazards.

Many people argue, "But those few little pieces I have are hardly worth insuring," and perhaps they are not. It depends upon the type of collection, whether it can be duplicated, how much money it represents, and so on. It would be rather extravagant to insure separately a collection of trade cards or post cards which can be bought in lots for as low as a dollar. They may be just as important to the collector as a row of historical flasks, but they are not irreplaceable, and until they move into the one-of-a-kind bracket do not represent a big outlay of funds. Be satisfied for the time being to include them as hobby material under your Dwelling-house Comprehensive Policy at no extra cost. But if you are going in for something that costs money or if you expect to move from the ranks of beginning collector to advanced collector, you are going to become more discriminative and what you buy is going to cost more. Perhaps you are a china enthusiast but right now are buying ironstone in one of the later patterns, say Bamboo or Wheat, but soon you go on to Gaudy Ironstone and maybe from there to the Imari English patterns of Spode or Worcester, or you progress from late Spode Tower to early Spode Tower. In each case your collection becomes more valuable and before you know it it may be worth a sum that will surprise you.

Some collectors labor under the belief that the dwelling-house policy they carry on their household goods chiefly for fire, and certain natural hazards covers the pieces they may have acquired in collecting and is therefore sufficient. If it has an extended coverage endorsement, it may include other things such as theft and loss from explosion, windstorm, riot, hail, smoke, etc., and it will, to a certain extent, and under certain circumstances, take care of your collection, but only under general classifications as china and glassware, silver, linens, clothing, furniture, etc. There will be nothing to indicate that the things so insured in your collection have any *special* value over the over-all valuation set for that classification in the policy. Often this valuation is set low because many people feel they cannot afford full coverage on their household goods and personal possessions. They gamble, feeling that nowadays with good fire protection, more prevention because of new building materials and household fire-fighting equipment, a home will seldom be burned out. Their main concern is still fire. So they compromise with a policy that only partially covers the value of the contents of the house. If there is a collection involved, it comes under that inadequate coverage and if something happens to it only a part of its value can be redeemed.

Some years back it was not possible to get special coverage for your collection or hobby. Now there is a policy designed expressly for the purpose. It is called a Fine Arts Policy, which may be written separately or made part of your Personal Property or Homeowner's Policy. Under a Fine Arts Policy every piece of value is separately recorded and evaluated for all risks subject to certain exclusions (more about this later), and including breakage if you wish to pay the extra premium.

What does an insurance company consider as fine arts? This is the term which they apply to paintings, etchings, pictures, tapestries, valuable rugs, statuary, bronzes, marbles, antique silver, antique furniture, rare books, manuscripts, porcelains, rare glass, and bric-a-brac of rarity, historical value, or artistic merit. Most collections would come under this definition, especially the last part, which can be widely inclusive. If you have any doubt whether your collection meets the fine-arts requirements your insurance representative can set you right. Sometimes the Fine Arts Policy is defined as a protection for your "hobby."

So now let's see what this sort of policy will do over and

above the other insurance. It covers against all risks of loss or damage or theft, which does not have to be burglary with forceful entry, and from almost any cause such as vandalism or malicious mischief, trapped birds, falling tree limbs, collapse of part of the house. It covers damage from landslide. It insures a scheduled piece in transit to or from exhibits or while out on loan, or newly purchased articles shipped to you or expressed by you after purchasing (providing they are scheduled). But to collect transit insurance you must be prepared to employ competent packers. It also protects the scheduled items from breakage by collision, derailment, or turnover of conveyance. It will take care of marring and scratching under these various circumstances. However, if you feel that breakage from other causes not mentioned in your policy could endanger a very fragile collection, you can obtain a breakage insurance that covers it for as little as fifteen cents per $100 worth of insurance.

There are some things no policy will cover, and it is good to know them. One is that articles are not covered while in a national or international exhibit or fair unless a special endorsement is requested. This is not too apt to concern the beginning collector but it is well to know about it. It does not cover damage from vermin, which means not only rats and mice but the squirrel that gets into your attic or comes down your chimney. It does not cover damage from moths. It does not take into consideration damage done during restoration. A chair is sent to be recaned, let's say. During the work a rung or leg is broken. You cannot claim damage on that. No claim can be made for natural wear and tear owing to age, such as fading, crackling, breaks or holes in a fabric, peeling of lacquer, brown spots on paper or linen, and so on. Nor does it cover damages caused by extremes of temperature or dampness (unless occasioned by other allowable causes such as rain or snow). If you find your old coverlet a mass of mildew after a summer in a trunk in the cellar, you can't put in a claim for it with the insurance company. There are also the unexpected but possible hazards such as damage from hostile action in peace or war, from atomic weapons, insurrection, rebellion, usurped power, seizure under customs or quarantine or any other government confiscation, risks of smuggling, all of which the insurance companies do not recognize. If your property is located in the Gulf states windstorms, tornados, and hurricanes must be excluded or an additional charge paid for the coverage.

How will you set up this sort of Fine Arts Policy? It is assumed you will have the help of a broker or agent but it is up to you what you will include in your separate schedule and how you will evaluate it. Each item of worth should be listed separately except in certain instances where the whole collection can be listed as one item. Take buttons. It would be almost impossible to list several hundred buttons many of which would cost well under a dollar a piece. So an approximate value can be put on the collection as a whole based on the records which we hope you have kept as you bought them. If there are some especially valuable ones they could be listed separately, or they could be grouped in categories such as calicoes, militaries, Wedgwood, jeweled, paperweight, inlay, etc. The same procedure would hold for other small collectibles.

Now as to valuation. Who is to say what the value is? If you are collecting in a high-bracket category such as Gaudy Dutch, guns, mechanical banks, Meissen figures, Battersea enamels (none of which the beginning collector is apt to start with), you should employ an appraiser to go over your list or your stock, someone who is professional and acceptable to the insurance company and whose word will stand if catastrophe descends upon your collection. Many companies have their own appraisers or can refer you to one they trust. It is not likely, however, that the beginning collector will want to go to the expense of an appraisal if he can avoid it. Of course if the beginner starts out with an inherited collection of size and value, as often happens, it might be well to call in an appraiser if it has not already been done by the estate of the deceased for distribution or inheritance-tax purposes.

But as a rule if you are a beginner you should be able to evaluate your own pieces starting with the prices you paid for them. If you bought the piece yesterday or a few weeks ago or maybe months ago the buying price is probably the value to put on the schedule—unless you paid too much for it, or maybe even got it at a bargain. In either case a study of the market, the prices quoted in ads or in the shops or at sales will give you the right valuation. If you bought the piece five years ago or maybe only two years back it may now be worth more than you paid for it. Or perhaps the piece was given to you and you have no idea of its worth. Then you will have to go digging for the current market price, of which more to follow.

Now remember values do not stand still. Prices of certain collectibles have risen like leavened dough because of the great demand for them. Six lion glass goblets bought at a country sale twenty years ago for 35 cents a piece today will be worth from $8.00 to $10.00 a piece. Only a few years ago interesting character bottles could be picked up for a few dollars a piece. Today you can pay as high as $25.00 for certain bottles. Your schedule should represent as far as possible the worth of the piece today. For this reason your schedule should be examined regularly and revised at least once a year. With prices for antiques moving upward so rapidly you will be cheating yourself if you don't, because only your scheduled value will be accepted. A friend of mine learned this lesson the hard way. She had valued a pair of Louis Philippe period French bisque figurines at $30.00 because they had been a gift, brought from abroad, and she had no idea of the price good bisque was bringing. Before she could investigate or change her evaluation they were stolen from her. She got her $30.00 but found out to her chagrin that figures like hers were selling in the New York shops for at least $75.00.

It is also important that you remove from the list anything that you sell or give away or trade, and just as important to notify the company of any additions to the schedule as you acquire them, although they will be automatically protected for ninety days if they do not exceed 25 per cent of the total amount of the policy. While there is no rebate in the premium for claims made during the life of a policy unless premium insurance has been purchased, there is additional insurance for new objects added.

This whole business of evaluation brings up one of the most baffling problems to the beginning collector. How much is it worth? It is the question I am asked most often, and it is the hardest to answer. The one honest answer, which gets no one anywhere, is that it is worth exactly what someone at the moment will pay for it. There is no way to set uniform prices on antiques, for they are not production items. Each piece is a rule unto itself. They are not subject to any fair-trade rulings. The fact that they do operate in a comparatively narrow range within a certain area is rather surprising. Of course the competition between the shops does act as some kind of a stabilizer. If you find ten-inch tea-leaf plates in one shop for about $3.00 a piece you'll find six other shops nearby charging about the same, $2.50 to $3.50. And so if you happen to have some tea-leaf plates to put on your Fine Arts Policy schedule and don't know what they are worth you visit six shops and strike an average. This might include the dealer who likes to keep his price up and wait for the right customer or the other kind who prefers a big turnover with smaller profit, but if you shop around enough you'll begin to get the price pattern. That is what the price guides do. They can be quite helpful in determining value but don't treat them as Bibles. Remember they cover the whole country and arrive at their prices by striking an average.

There is quite a discrepancy in prices between different parts of the country. West Coast prices are supposed to be higher than on the East Coast, although this is debated.

However, it is a fact that transportation of antiques across the country does add to the cost, aside from the fact that there is more abundance of old things in the East to call upon. One dealer who spends six months of the year in Vermont loads up her station wagon and treks west for the other six months, unloading the things she knows Californians like at much higher prices. There are northern dealers who move part or all of their stock South for the winter months, where they not only do more business but get higher prices from the resorters. A Pennsylvania woman keeps two shops, one in her own small town and another in her holiday cottage by the sea where she catches the idle and moneyed vacationer. Where there is a concentration of money, as in the big cities, prices will be higher.

So there are many things to consider in setting a value on the pieces you own. You would be foolish to put it too low simply because you were canny enough to have picked up the piece in some out-of-the-way place. On the other hand, it is not good business to put it too high. You might be challenged. Because those Christmas-tree lights you bought for $2.00 a piece, the price in most shops, happen to have been tagged $8.00 in a smart Madison Avenue shop does not mean you can accept that as a true value. Be as honest as you can with an eye on the replacement value of the piece if you had to go out and buy it that day.

One thing to keep in mind is that prices are based on proof pieces, things without defects. If what you have bought is not perfect but is still worth declaring on your fine-arts schedule, it is better to state the condition of it, marking *not proof* against the item and adjusting the price to fit. Then if anything happens nobody can accuse you of claiming an exorbitant value for something that was not perfect. Thus on my own list I have itemized a marked Bennington coachman bottle at $15.00 because one toe is broken and the hat slightly chipped. If perfect, I would have claimed much more. If a thing has been mended professionally and perhaps invisibly, the value comes closer to proof, though experts can usually detect mending of any kind. The value will all depend upon the piece. Something very fine and very rare will hold up in value even when damaged or mended. You can see cracked pieces in many museum collections.

There is usually a clause in a policy that takes care of pairs and sets. This is because one of a matched pair or a piece in a matched set is worth more than the same piece singly. In other words, a pair is worth more than twice what each piece would be if found by itself. If a dealer can be persuaded to break a pair or a set he will ask much more proportionately for the single piece. And so the insurance company takes this into consideration. If one piece of a pair or a set is broken or stolen or damaged they consider the pair or set incomplete and its worth shrunken. They will do one of two things, they will pay you the full price of the set and claim the remaining piece or pieces, or let you keep the undamaged pieces and give you a commensurate higher price for the one that was stolen or damaged. Usually the claimant prefers the latter type of settlement if he feels he can replace the missing piece eventually. But be sure you have perfect matches and be sure to list them as pairs or sets, as for instance, "Matched pair of Sheffield candlesticks," or "Three-piece matched tea set in rose medallion." Then you have nothing to worry about if calamity strikes.

And so what this all boils down to is this: Will it pay to take out Fine Arts insurance if you have only a few good antique pieces either in or out of your collection? You may feel that you do not have enough things of value to warrant the expense—and you may be right. But this protection does not cost a terribly high price in dollars and cents for your peace of mind. The cost will vary depending upon the base rate determined by the insurance code for locality, etc. But just to get a rough idea of the cost of a Fine Arts Policy combined with a Personal Property or Homeowner's Policy let's say $6,500 might be the evaluation of your household and personal possessions; then you add to that $3,500 for the fine-arts items, making $10,000 in all. If you think this example is above average, just sit down and itemize everything you possess. The sum will surprise you. For the above valuation the premium on a three-year basis—which you would be wise to take as there is some saving—might run to about $208. This brings the average yearly premium to only $70.00, the price of just one stolen Staffordshire-type luster-headed doll, or half the price of a Mount Washington peach-blow vase. Of course a separate Fine Arts Policy would be considerably less, as this figure represents coverage for everything in your house, and if computed separately the Fine Arts floater would be only a fraction of the $70.00.

The best course to pursue, however, in determining whether you should take out such a protective policy and for how much is to consult a reliable broker or the agent of a company that handles such things. Some companies are better equipped for this kind of insurance than others. When you find the right broker, show him your inventory and get estimates on coverage and premiums. When you get the policy, *be sure to read the fine print* and be sure breakage has been included on breakable items.

And above all, whether you insure your collection or not, do keep a record of your purchases, the date bought, where bought, and the price paid. Someday you may need that information and it does give you a feeling of satisfaction and perhaps even justification for spending money you might have been feeling guilty about. Investment is a much better word than extravagance when it is applied to antiques.

9.

ANTIQUES AS AN INVESTMENT

IT would be the exceptional person who would start a collection with only its investment value in mind. There are some who may not think of it at all, others who are aware of it as a possible side benefit from a pleasurable avocation, and still others who use it as an alibi or excuse for their spending. But the fact remains that every *good* collection can be an investment for future realization. Whether it is on a long-term basis or a short-term depends upon what you collect. There are some pieces in immediate demand that you can turn over for a profit an hour after you buy them. This happens often at sales. A bidder who has lost out to you for some reason or other, while he was at lunch or not paying attention or because he did not realize what he was passing up, approaches you and asks if you want to sell the piece. If you are not too anxious to hold it, you may yield to a little pressure and make a quick profit, but if the piece means anything to you as a collectible it would be foolish to do so.

Long-term investment, however, is a different thing. It means looking into the future many years ahead with the idea that what you have is bound to increase in value which either you or your heirs can take advantage of. Even some things of little importance will season over the years and acquire value if they are "salted down" and forgotten as moneymakers. Most collections even in a short time will be worth more than you paid for them if you bought wisely. However, in selling they may have to be broken up and sold piece by piece. Not many people want to go out and buy a collection intact. This applies, of course, to collections of recognized antiques in good taste, those that will not deteriorate over the years. It does not apply to fads or items popular for only a short time. For such things it would be wiser to take a short-term profit while you can, because it is such trivial collectibles that will go off in price first if the market falls or the fad dies out. It would take a great personal distress to cause someone to sell out his collection of Queen Anne furniture but he could let a collection of taffeta or carnival glass go without a qualm. The good things, the old china, glass, silver, and furniture, will hold up come what may.

What is going to happen to the antique picture? Is the cream off in collecting? Will the collectors of today reap the same profits as the collectors of fifty years ago? It would take more of a prophet than I am to say. However, I will say that although the original sources of antiques in this country are gradually drying up, there will still be redistribution to consider. Collections, unless they are given to museums, don't stay intact forever.

Right now we are riding along with inflation so that the antique business is good. Will it keep up? Will the market fall? It could in the same way that any market can fall the minute supply exceeds demand. This can happen in the field of antiques when some major economic catastrophe forces people to the market place in need of money. In this era of prosperity and rising prices we can't envision it. No slight recession, however, is going to cause the holder of good "blue-chip" antiques to unload because he knows that they have a built-in value that will survive everything but an atom bomb. He'd be more likely to borrow on his insurance or other securities first. Unloading under personal economic stress, often piece by piece, brings good antiques into the market which right now can absorb it.

There are besides a great upheaval in national economy other things that can depress the market for short periods or in certain lines. Reproductions can wreak havoc. Because of them people shy off from buying the old as well as the new. There is too much around of a certain thing and the old pieces lose their novelty. A violin flask, once a find for a bottle collector, is now seen in every gift shop. The influx of foreign imports has done a lot to depress prices in certain lines. Cranberry glass, for instance, once a choice item for collectors, has been brought over in such quantities from England that interest in it has slackened. The same goes for bisque, plaster ornaments, and onion Meissen. Yet, and this is important to show how fickle the market can be, interest in foreign stuff is reported to be dying off as the taste of collectors switches back to Americana.

Another thing that can depress the market, temporarily at least, is the publicized story of a sale where prices were low. For some reason prices did not meet the market or top it and so the whole picture changes and prices dip generally. This happened at a recent sale of fine clocks when a banjo clock, possibly Willard, in excellent running condition, brought only $90.00 and a Terry shelf clock circa 1830 brought but $32.50. The reason was not apparent, but the result was. It will take a bit of time for the depressing effect to wear off. However, it worked out well for the collectors who bought them. They will merely have to bide their time until the market comes back, as it will.

There is another possibility in the halt of high prices. Some dealers are claiming that certain pieces have "priced themselves out of the market." Such pieces are moving very slowly because even the well-heeled buyers are balking at the prices. This may slow up buying for a time, but eventually as antiques ride along with the inflation even these higher-priced items will be absorbed.

In looking at antiques as investments we find they follow a pattern common to investments generally. When a new sales-man goes out to sell bonds or investment stocks he is indoc-trinated with the principle of the *triangle* by which every good investment is measured. The three sides of the triangle are labeled *security, yield* (computed from interest and buy-ing price), and *marketability*. Seldom are the three sides equal. The base represents the strongest feature. Security means the quality of the investment, what stands back of it in the way of history, management, physical holdings, record of earnings. New issues that have not had time to prove them-selves may be short on security and so will have to make it up in yield. The better the offering the lower the yield, as wit-ness United States Government bonds. But unless a stock can be sold easily either by listing on one of the boards or in an active private market it can be a risk. Higher interest rates help marketability as well as does the soundness of an invest-ment. So marketability is important.

Now let's look at antiques. Security here would mean, of course, the accumulation of only good, authentic pieces. It would outlaw everything that is not proof, admitting recon-ditioned or mended pieces only in exceptional circumstances. It would most certainly outlaw anything that was reproduced or about which there was doubt. So it would seem that the collector with an eye on the long-term investment value of his collection should make very sure that he is getting the best his money will buy. He may be tempted to fill in with chipped or cracked pieces which he can get cheap, and if he doesn't expect too much of them they will do until he can find better. Later he will replace them with pieces in mint condition, if he can. Oddities and rarities may be an exception to this rule. In selling off imperfect pieces one is never sure of getting even what one paid for them, although the tendency today is to overlook minor chips and scratches because of the scarcity of mint pieces. This is especially true where the history of a piece makes it important. You might wait years to pick up a perfect Stiegel sugar bowl but you would scarcely turn down one with a crack in the bottom. Museums have had to settle for such things. However, if you are buying with the investment value of your collection in mind, go easy on imperfect goods. Examine everything carefully. Hold china and glass up to the light to spot imperfections or mended breaks. Run your fingers over all edges. Sometimes edges have been ground down, but if you know your stuff you will recognize it. For instance, you should know that if you are being offered a set of cut-glass "old-fashioneds" that they must have been cut down from a set of nicked tumblers. Old-fashioneds do not go back to the cut-glass era.

Be sure that what you have are true mates if you are buying pairs, that the bottle or decanter or cruet has the right stopper, the tea caddy the right canisters, the cruet stand the right bottles and jars, the piece of furniture the right brasses, or the chest the right hinges, and if not that the price reflects the discrepancy. It may be wise not to pass up a piece that is not complete because often the rest of it can be found, say the proper lid for a Three-Faces compote. This searching can be part of the fun.

Now let's look at this frightening business of reproductions, for it is frightening not only to the beginner but to the dealers as well, for it is scaring off many customers from buying the things they know are being reproduced. Now no reputable dealer is going to stock reproductions unless he honestly tells you so. There is a growing tendency for even old, established shops to put in reproductions of familiar items and mix them with their old stock. They do not sell them as old, but they feel such things fill up when antique stocks run low. They say the public wants them, particularly the young marrieds, that if they can't get the originals they satisfy themselves with good copies. There is no reason why they shouldn't buy reproductions if they want them, but personally I think the place for them is the gift shop or the decorating shop, not the antique shop. They should be kept as far as possible away from the antique market. Too many misunderstandings and mistakes can be made by mixing the old and the new. It takes courage for a dealer to say when a customer waxes enthusiastic over a milk-white butter dish, "That isn't old." If you know your dealer, you may run no risk in feeling your way among the reproductions, but if he is unknown to you how are you to be sure if you pick up an Uncle Sam bank dusty and rusted even to its inside screws that it is not an original? The dealer may shrug off your question with "I bought it for an old one," but if you happen to know that this bank has been reproduced by the hundreds you better put it down and move on.

It is contended that modern reproductions will not fool the initiated. There are always things to give the new piece away, color, weight, size, slight variations of shape or pattern, finish of the edges, etc. But until you have handled a great many pieces of the old it is not always easy to spot the new. Even dealers admit they can be fooled. But a good dealer will stand back of his wares, and if he unwittingly sells a reproduction for a genuine piece he will make it good or take it back. That is the best guarantee that any buyer can ask.

Much is being done to smoke out the reproductions that are put on the market if not primarily to deceive the buyer at least to confuse him. The magazines carry articles giving news of recent reproductions. Follow them carefully. Dealers watch the catalogues of known sources. Books have been written full of information on how to spot the "wrong" pieces, notably Ruth Webb Lee's *Antique Fakes and Reproductions,* *Antique Fakes and Their Detection* by Raymond E. Yates, *Fakes, a Handbook for Collectors* by Kurz, *Care and Repair of Antiques* by Thomas Ormsbee, and *Early American Pattern Glass* by Alice Hewlitt Metz. The *Warman Price Guide* usually stars pieces that are being reproduced. Armed with such warnings a collector should be able to steer clear of the fakes. But the best way is to learn for yourself. Study and look and feel. The advanced collector rubs his fingers over a piece of heavy glass and says, "This is not old." He can tell by the feel alone. A good silversmith can spot an old hallmark that has been almost invisibly soldered into an alien piece, something the amateur might miss.

It has been suggested that there should be a law requiring reproductions to carry the date of manufacture. It would seem like a good idea although the suggestion has been hotly debated. There would be ways, no doubt, to get around such a law as there is with everything else. But other regulations have worked, such as the McKinley Bill in 1891 that required the country of origin to be stamped upon every import and which is something of a guide for gatherers of antiques. Marking reproductions would certainly be a great help in establishing authenticity.

It is sad to relate that not always even with professional guidance can you be sure that what you have is genuine. A silver pitcher identified by one of the country's biggest and most reliable silversmiths as a valuable Georgian piece was rejected by a confrere as a modern fake. Whom to believe? No authority is infallible. Almost every big collection that comes on the market discloses some "mistakes." Unfortunately this rejection is often inspired by professional jealousy or a desire to express authoritative knowledge. Sour grapes, in other words. But the authority with integrity will be the first to bow his head when he is wrong. So don't feel too bad if you find you have a black sheep in your collection. The main thing is not to walk into an area where reproductions are rampant until you know what you are doing.

So much for the *security* of your investment. What about the *marketability?* Certainly you cannot realize upon your investment until you sell it and you won't sell it if there is no buyer for it. As the antique market stands today there would seem to be a buyer for almost everything. But talk to the dealers. They can point to areas where interest has slackened off. Popularity waxes and wanes in certain lines. Not so long ago a dealer told me in connection with a rather large and selective collection of Tobies which we both knew, "Mr. C wants to sell out but he's going to have a hard time doing it, especially as a collection. He wants too much and right now Tobies are a slow item. Of course some dealer may take them and put them away for a while." This analysis might have been true only of a certain locality, but it is quoted to show that the market varies even if built-in value does not.

Take the man who had inherited a fine old Dutch *kas,* a really beautiful piece, dated 1776 and signed with the original owner's name. He had to sell it because he had no room for it. But he could not get rid of it. Only a museum would pay him what he was asking for it—not an exorbitant price by any means, but he could not find a museum that was in the market for such a piece. As for the dealers, they shied off because it was too large for the modern home, seven feet high, seven feet wide, and more than two feet deep. In spite of its age and fine condition, it was too hard to sell. One dealer with two in his shop was willing to part with them for far less than the owner wanted. So here was a case of a fine piece going begging because there was no market for it. The unfortunate thing is that somewhere someone would probably have been happy to find such a piece, but how to contact such a buyer? The owner finally decided to "lend" it to a small museum while waiting for someone to see it and buy it.

Another woman has been trying for years to get rid of a very fine Indian cashmere shawl which she had appraised at what seemed a very high sum, a "museum piece," as she was told. She won't give it up for less even though it cost her nothing. But she has yet to find a museum or an individual collector who will give her her price or who wants it at any price. Marketability depends not only on the character of the piece but on contact between a seller and a buyer, and sometimes this is very hard to negotiate. Advertising is, of course, the obvious answer, but even then, for an unusual thing, the right person might not see the ad.

A friend of mine held on for years to a series of Japanese prints which she had picked up very cheap. She felt they had come off an old screen and discovered that they told a story and were complete. She tried to dispose of them through many avenues but because she could not put any identifying name or period to them she could arouse no interest. Finally in a period of personal depression she was forced to let them go for almost nothing. There is no doubt that the value was there but the marketability was not.

Now what about the *yield*—in this case the profit? As has been said over and over the value of most antiques does increase with age. All kinds of stories are told to point this up. For instance, it is said that when Harry Peters, the Currier and Ives expert, began to collect his lithographs about fifty years ago be picked them up for 25 cents and 50 cents apiece. Today, unless you are lucky enough to find some buried in an old house or unidentified in a pile of old papers, they will cost you from a possible low of $5.00 or $6.00 to a high of $4,500, with many titles in the hundreds. An investment of $100 back there in 1910 would have paid off ten, twenty, or maybe thirty times, even if you had not bought the rarest items. But comparing the dollar value then and now you would have to write off probably half of your profits and would you have held on to them for fifty years? Also would you have been as canny as Mr. Peters? It was his study and research when joined with other enthusiasts that gave the prints standing as a collectible and settled their comparative values. Can stories like this be repeated today? What is there to be bought for 50 cents today that will be worth $500 fifty years from now? Maybe not much. Maybe we have milked the market dry. But there are still some things that the canny collector will recognize as being worth the buying now.

A collector who went in for colored tumblers thirty years

ago because "they were pretty" now discovers that she has in her collection of 150 many in the various art glass groups that might run as high as $75.00. Just by holding on to something she liked she can now reap a beautiful profit.

It is always interesting to compare today's prices with lists of ten or even a few years ago. Invariably they will be higher. Bankers will tell you that money invested at 3 per cent compound interest will double in seventeen years, at 6 per cent in twelve years. Many antiques double in value in less. All right, you say, but suppose I put the same money into a piece of property in a boom area or buy some good blue-chip stocks? I not only have the prospect of appreciation but a return on my money in rental or interest while I hold them. True, but you can enjoy and use your antiques while you hold them, and in the end their greater increase in value will probably more than make up the loss in interest. It costs money to hold property, and stocks move up and down with much variation in dividends.

While an antique does not yield cash interest while it ages, it does yield other things that can sometimes be turned into money. Many collectors make their collections pay for themselves. They rent them for commercial displays. They may lend them as fund-raising exhibits for charitable or community projects and thus use them as a substitute for a heavy cash contribution. They may even be able to write off certain expenses entailed in lending them in the contribution deduction bracket of their income-tax return, things such as transportation, packing, insurance, etc. When a collector begins to accumulate knowledge about his hobby, he can often find speaking engagements at clubs and schools especially if he has a good collection of slides to accompany his talk. True he may be asked to do this gratis, and if he feels so inclined it is a gracious thing to do. But experience soon shows that it is hard to say yes to one group and no to another, so that it is better to charge a fee regardless and gear it to the financial status of the group. Again if a collector has a way with words he can turn his knowledge into articles for papers or magazines. So all these things can be considered as part of the *yield* on your investment in antiques.

There may be some times when you decide to sell some pieces without waiting for the long-term profit. If so, remember you must declare your profit in your income tax either as a short-term capital gain if you have held the piece less than six months or a long-term capital gain if for more than six months. Canny collectors who do not want to add to their income in this way often resort to swapping among themselves so that no cash passes to be declared in the way of profit. The profit will show up only when the piece taken in swap is sold.

Right here I must advise the collector to keep records of his purchases, the date bought, the price paid, and the source, and with it any other costs for transportation, mending, refinishing, etc. If it costs you $5.00 to get that old sofa home from the sale that is really part of the cost. It does not take much work to enter each piece in a small ledger or notebook the minute you have bought it. There are even some books printed for such records. Often at sales you will see a buyer with his notebook and pencil ready to enter everything he buys. He doesn't trust to memory. This is the only proof you may have to offer if the time comes to dispose of a piece. It's a good plan to carry a small memo book with you for the purpose at all times.

Starting a Business

One way to realize profit from your investment is to use your collection as a starting point for opening a business in antiques. You do not necessarily have to put your collection on sale. If it is a substantial one evaluated by a reliable appraiser, well insured, and with no prospect of deterioration, many banks will accept it as collateral for what they might call a "token loan" or a chattel mortgage. It would all depend upon your locality, the way the bankers feel about antiques, and your own reputation as a reliable person. Bankers are hard-boiled people, they have to be, and often they cannot be persuaded that certain things make good collateral. If you were lucky enough to strike a bank that I know where the president has deliberately filled his own home with antiques purely on an investment basis you might have no trouble. You might be required to keep the collection intact until you had repaid at least part of the loan. But this will work out all right because it can be used for window dressing and the money you borrow to buy new stock. Also it establishes you as a specialist, and your best procedure might be to keep on specializing in it. You have collected, let's say, majolica for years, so you go in heavily for it because you know it.

But just because you know your antiques does not say that you will make a success of the business of selling them. However, you can learn. There have been several good books written on how to start an antique business, such as *Antiques for Profit* by Frank Ormston, *How to Price Antiques* by Larry Freeman, *The Antique Shop* by Louise Shepard. These are all sound and go into the fine points of financing, pricing, selling, etc. They would certainly be worth buying and reading if you have a shop in mind. Talking to other dealers will help you avoid making major mistakes. On the other hand, you may prefer to do your selling entirely by mail (see Chapter 4) or by exhibiting at antique shows or simply by appointment in your home. It will all depend upon the size and character of what you plan to sell. And even with a business you can keep on with your private collecting.

So often when you visit a shop you will find the salable articles grouped by themselves, but if you have made a hit with the dealer or have come to know him well you will be taken into another part of the house to see the things he has kept for himself, either because he cannot bear to part with them or because he wants to hold them for a higher market. Sometimes this is a ruse to make it hard for you to buy, to make you do a little coaxing, and give him a chance to set the price for whatever he feels the transaction will bear. But not always. Very often it is just because he wants to share his fine things with you like any other collector.

A collection is a very useful slide board for easing into an antique business. It gives you a chance to go slowly and buy cannily until you learn the price ranges not only in your specialized field but in other lines and until you begin to find out what will sell readily and what won't.

It is often possible to buy out a small business, lock, stock, and barrel. If you contemplate doing this be sure to find out the real reason why the owner is giving it up. Don't just take "illness" for an answer. It may be a bad place for an antique business, or the new highway may be going to by-pass it, or he may have a bad reputation which you will have to live down, or he may have been loaded with a lot of unsalable stuff for that part of the country. If the business has been successful, you will have to pay accordingly, not only for the stock but for good will. But it is possible, if you have the

know-how, to build up a small, unostentatious business which
you may pick up if not for the proverbial song at least reasonably. It is often better to start with a ready-made business like
this than to have to stock from scratch, antiques being so hard
to find today. It is the old, established dealers who are making
the money because they have been buying longer and may
still have backlogs of pieces bought before small pickings and
high prices began.

It is still possible to pick up merchandise at the country
sales, although in some areas they are so patronized by other
dealers and wealthy buyers there will be no bargains. If you
are thinking of stocking a shop, however, you can afford to
buy many things that are not in such great demand. Last
summer in Vermont I saw a young woman doing just this at
a country sale sponsored by the local DAR. It was evident
she did not know too much about antiques, and talking to
her I discovered she was just starting a business. But she kept
picking up things the other women didn't want, a Bennington spittoon, a small horsehide trunk, part of a Paisley shawl,
and so on. She kept an eye on the auctioneer, who had appar-
ently a friendly interest in her. If he nodded when she bid,
she kept on, and often he was able to throw the bid her way.
She'll get along.

There are dealers who wholesale to other dealers. In stocking a shop it might pay to do some business with them. You'll
get enough of a discount to make the purchase worth-while.
Many dealers get their stock from "pickers," people who
make a business of going around the country finding things
no one else could find or take the time to find. They get into
old houses and stores and spot small dealers on back roads
from which they may buy wholesale. Such a picker may come
in with ten glass lamps which he can sell cheap if you take the

lot. But you better know your picker and where the stuff comes from. You don't want to get into trouble with stolen stuff or reproductions. Many dealers refuse to buy from unknown sellers for this reason.

Dealers make a practice of going from one section of the country to another to do their buying in cheaper areas. Remember the story of the Vermont woman (Chapter 8) who loaded up her station wagon and trekked across country to sell her wares in California? Most of what she gathered up came from the Vermont dealers and was bought out of season while prices were low.

It is a fact that much of a dealer's stock comes from other dealers. Sometimes it seems like a puss-in-the-corner game and you wonder where the antiques really originate and how long they have been traveling about passing from hand to hand. But it can be seen why it is this way. In the first place, finding antiques "at source" gets harder every day. Today's problem for any dealer is to replace the things he sells and to face the fact that each time he buys he must pay more. A dealer has a number of calls for, let's say, satin glass, and wakes up to the fact that he hasn't a piece in the shop. So he goes shopping for it to other dealers who may have more pieces or less calls for it. Each dealer knows what he can sell. He knows what customers are waiting for what. So he goes out looking for certain pieces for his private collectors. He will get the dealer discount, which varies from 10 per cent to 20 per cent of the retail price. It gives him a chance to make a small profit fast or he may even be able to up the price a bit because he knows the particular customer will pay it. He keeps the customer happy, makes a sale, and a profit, if not a big one. If he is price-conscious and knows his antiques, he may do very well by buying from others who do not know as much.

So if you are thinking of capitalizing on your collection by starting a business, give all these things thought before you decide definitely where and how to start. Certainly your shop should *look* well stocked when you open up. That is where your own collection will come in handy. Nothing is surer to turn business away than a skimpily stocked shop, with a handful of things looking lost in an almost empty room. The word gets around. "Yes, he has some nice things but there really isn't much there. Hardly worth stopping." One way to get around this is to take things on consignment. Let your friends or people you know put in things they want to sell and charge them a 20 per cent commission for selling. It helps to fill up. You may even find your family or friends will *lend* you things to tide you over until you become established.

So be sure to stock up first in some way to make a good showing and make up your mind that you will probably have to throw back profits into the business for a long time. While the antique business isn't what it was back in the "good old days," when things were easier to find, buying is good. There are still shops opening every day and they seem to make money. So why not you?

10.

FAMOUS COLLECTIONS

IN every state of the Union there are museums, private and state-owned, operated by historical societies or educational institutions, supported by commercial concerns, that devote themselves entirely or partly to the preservation of Americana. Add to these the restored houses, the special rooms in other historic buildings, and you have a wide viewing choice for the collector to study the thing he is most interested in. When it is remembered that large private collections not available to the public are often lent or finally given to the museums, it enlarges the field. Also there are "traveling collections" that get before the public from time to time at shows, exhibits, etc.

Museums seem to concentrate along the eastern seaboard where the supply of early things brought over or used by the first colonies was greatest. But in every part of the country there are collections that reflect the origins and customs of its settlers. Thus in New Orleans and along the Gulf you will find the French and Spanish influence, in Texas and New Mexico the Mexican-Spanish, in California the Spanish of the old mission days, in Wisconsin and Minnesota the German and Scandinavian. In the western states cattle raising and gold mining produced their own mementoes of the past for interested collectors, and all through the West museums are full of Indian items, baskets, blankets, pottery, as well as the arrowheads and other artifacts of the region. Coming back to Ohio you will find relics of the early glassmaking that moved on from Pittsburgh, and in West Virginia pottery fanning out from the Pennsylvania and New Jersey potteries. Marine and whaling museums along the seaboard offer the collector of nautical items much to look at and study.

General collections of Americana in the big groups of glass, china, silver, pewter, prints, furniture abound all over the country in art museums, historical societies, and college and university museums; they are worth visiting by anyone interested in the collecting of American antiques. But as far as specialized collections go, these are more apt to be found in the hands of private collectors and except on occasions when they are open to the public for things like Open House Days, exhibits for charity, etc., are not available for viewing. Here and there, however, in the exhibits open to the public there can be found special collections within the generalized areas of classification. These are the ones listed below. I have arranged them by states so that they will be easier to locate.

Arkansas

Lonsdale Museum, Lonsdale (near Hot Springs National Park)
    Lonsdale Collection of Coin Glass
Museum of Arkansas State College, Jonesboro
    American glass
Fine Arts Museum, Little Rock
    American glass
Albert Pike Museum, Winslow
    Pressed glass

California

Early Colonial Drugstore, 701 South St. Andrew's Place, Los
Angeles
  Apothecary items
Siskiyou Co. Historical Society, Yerka
  Dolls
De Saisset Art Gallery and Museum, Santa Clara
  Shawls
  Miniatures
  Steins
  Clocks
  Mission items, vestments, etc.
  Indian items

Colorado

Colorado Springs Fine Arts Center—Taylor Museum
  Spanish-American religious art
Children's Museum—Denver
  Dolls
  Dollhouses

Connecticut

Just Buttons Museum—Southington
  Buttons
Toy Museum, Old Lyme
  Dolls
  Dollhouses and furniture
Colt Firearms Museum—Hartford
  Extensive collection of Colt revolvers
Clock and Watch Museum—Bristol
Connecticut State Museum—Hartford
  Buttons—90,000 in collection
Yale and Towne—Stamford
  Bailey Lock Collection (traveling exhibit)
Marine Historical Association—Mystic
  Scrimshaw
  Figureheads

Ship models
Whaling items
Ship prints and paintings
New Haven Colony Historical Society—New Haven
    Connecticut pewter
Lyman Allyn Museum—New London
    Dolls
    Toy furniture
Wadsworth Atheneum—Hartford
    Wallace Nutting furniture
Wesleyan University, Davison Art Center—Middletown
    English and American prints

Delaware

Winterthur Museum—Wilmington
    Silver
    Wills pewter
    Tucker china
    Painted tin
    Candy jars
    Brass candlesticks
    Chinese Export china
    Staffordshire pottery
    White salt-glaze stoneware
    Spatterware
    Child's furniture
    Sgraffito
    Slipware
    Chalkware
    Castleford pottery
    Frankliniana
    Liverpool tiles
    Whieldon
    Canary and silver luster
    Worcester china
    Chelsea
    Bristol

Quillwork
Delft
New England needlepoint
Textiles
Wallpapers
Carpets

Florida

Ringling Brothers Museum—Sarasota
    Circus items
    Magician's items
Art Studio, 555 S. W. First St.—Miami
    Famous Lithophane Collection of Dr. Edmond Beroud
Rollins College—Winter Park
    Dr. Eugene R. Smith Collection of Watch Keys
Lightner Museum of Hobbies—St. Augustine
    Buttons—uniform and costume

Illinois

Art Institute of Chicago
    Hester Bateman silver
    The Antiquarian Collection of American Silver
George F. Harding Museum—Chicago
    Firearms
    Cannons
    Ship models
    Musical instruments
Illinois State Museum of Natural History and Art—Springfield
    Coverlets
    Shawls
    Fans
    Clocks
Chicago Museum of Science and Industry
    Colleen Moore Collection of Miniaturia

Indiana

Lincoln National Life Foundation—Fort Wayne
    Lincolniana

Eli Lilly and Co.—Indianapolis
   Drugstore and medical items

Kansas

University of Kansas Museum of Art—Lawrence
M. Jones Collection of Timepieces

Kentucky

Barton Museum of Whiskey—Bardstown
   Licenses
   Bottles
   Advertising posters

Louisiana

Antoine's Restaurant—New Orleans
   Snail dishes
   Ash trays
State Museum—New Orleans (Cabildo and Pontalba Bldgs.)
   Glass
   Jewelry
   Costumes

Maine

Brick Store Museum—Kennebunkport
   Costumes
   Ship models
Colby College—Waterville
   American Heritage Collection of Folk Art (85 objects)
   Miller Library—25,000 maps

Maryland

Baltimore Museum of Art
   Baltimore silver
Peale Museum—Baltimore
   Hambleton Collection of Baltimore Views
Maryland Arms Collectors' Association—Baltimore
   Guns

United States Naval Academy—Annapolis
  Ship models
Mrs. Kay's Toll House (restaurant)—Silver Springs
  Nicholas Lutz glass
  Franklin Maxim plates and cups in Franklin Room
  Glass plates—made into window

Massachusetts

Beverly Historical Society—Beverly
  Ship models
  Pewter
  Embroideries
  Glass
  Porcelain
Old Dartmouth Historical Society and Whaling Museum—New
    Bedford
  Scrimshaw
  Dolls
  Whaling items
Plymouth Antiquarian Society—Plymouth
  Implements
  Old household items
  Dolls
  Period costumes
Museum of Fine Arts—Boston
  Miniatures
American Antiquarian Society—Worcester
  Early American portraits
  Staffordshire
  Bookplates
  Prints
  Lithographs
  Newspapers
  Almanacs
  Music
  Valentines
  Bookmarks

1,200 Cookbooks
Lithographs
More Collection of American Views on Staffordshire
Wenham Historical Association and Museum—Wenham
Dolls
Figurines
Children's Museum—Jamaica Plain
Dolls
Johnny Cake Hill Museum—New Bedford
Dolls
Essex Institute Salem
Buttons
Costumes
Silver
Pewter
Glass
China
Apothecary shop
Hammond Collection of Clocks
Rogers groups
Tools
Sewing machines
Typewriters
Franklin stoves
Pottery
Musical instruments
Agricultural instruments
Vaughn doll and toy house
Peabody Museum—Salem
75,000 maritime items
Old Sturbridge Village—Sturbridge
Pottery
Paperweights
Guns
Tools
Woodenware
Silver

Glass
Clocks
Silhouettes
Tintypes
Daguerreotypes
Signs
Fireboards
Fire buckets
Needlework pictures
Theorem pictures
Stencils
Instruction books
Drawing and painting instruments
Early American Industries—Worcester
Tools
Implements
Utensils
J. W. Higgins Museum, Worcester Pressed Steel Co.—Worcester
Iron items 1750–1850
Steel items
Gibson House—137 Beacon Street, Boston
Victoriana
State Street Trust Co.—Boston
Clipper ship items
John Green Chandler Memorial Museum—Lancaster
Paper dolls
Draper Museum of Looms and Spindles—Hopedale
Looms
Spinning wheels
Beauport—Gloucester
Pattern glass
Mary Earle Gould Museum—Worcester
Woodenware
Tin
The Sandwich Historical Society and Glass Museum—Sandwich
Sandwich glass
Miniature pieces

Michigan

The Henry Ford Museum—Dearborn
Vast collection of Americana in all fields
Furniture
Silver
Pewter
Glass
Pottery
Porcelain
Textiles
Clocks and watches
Lighting devices
Agricultural instruments
Iron
Music boxes
Dolls and toys
Miniatures
Guns
Needlework
Rugs
Household items
Paperweights
Prints
Decoys
Primitive sculpture
Treen
Folk painting
Bandboxes
Store items
Tools

Minnesota

Minneapolis Hennequin County Historical Society
Kitchen items (from pre-1858 Midwest kitchen)

Nebraska

Worp's Museum—Minden
   Items in Pioneer Village
Museum of The Union Pacific—Omaha
   Pioneer relics
   Weapons
   Railroad watches
   Flags
   Eagles
   Firemen's trumpets

New Hampshire

Goyette Museum of Americana—Peterborough
   Horse bridles and gear
   Metal soldiers
   Dolls
   Iron items
   Currier and Ives prints
   Flasks and bottles
   Liverpool ware
   Staffordshire
   Lowestoft
   Paperweights
   Buckles
   Pewter
   Brass
Currier Gallery of Art—Manchester
   Blown three-mold glass
   Pattern glass
   Wallpaper
   Embroideries
Doll Museum—Contoocook
   Dolls
   Dollhouses

New Jersey

Montclair Art Museum—Montclair
    Whitney Silver Collection
Salem County Historical Society—Salem
    Wistarburg glass
Kilmer Museum of Surgical Products, Johnson and Johnson—
    New Brunswick
    Drugstore and medical items

New Mexico

Museum of New Mexico Art Gallery—Santa Fe
    Spanish colonial items
    Bultos
    Santos
Harwood Foundation of the University of New Mexico—Taos
    Santos
    Primitive woodcarvings

New York

Brooklyn Museum
    American pewter
    Wedgwood
    Silver
Brooklyn Children's Museum
    Dolls
    Toys
Cooper Union—New York City
    Textiles
    Lace
    Embroidery
    Buttons
    Wallpaper
Museum of the City of New York
    Prints
    Maps
    Vehicles

Costumes
Magicians' wands
Costume accessories
Theater items
Toys
New York Historical Society—New York City
500 original Audubon water colors
Glass
Pottery
Silver
Pewter
Dolls
Toys
Lighting devices
Household items
Jenny Lind items
Ephemera
Military buttons
Shircliffe Collection, 10,000 menus
Metropolitan Museum—New York City
Glass
China
Costumes
Buttons—Kohn Collection
Chess pieces
Milk-glass animal covered dishes
Carl Dreppard Collection of Instruction Books
Pewter
Needlework pictures
New York University Gould Memorial Library—New York City
James Arthur Collection of Clocks and Watches
Scalamandre Museum of Textiles—New York City
Old textiles
Traphagen School of Fashion—New York City
Jewelry
Buttons
Dolls

Manikins and minikins
Figurines
Brasses
Textiles
Meissen
Rensselaer County Junior Museum—Troy
Mechanical banks
L. A. Johnson Country Store—Syracuse
Old country-store items
Musical Museum—Deansboro
Musical instruments
Phonographs
Pianos
Organs
Nickelodeons
Harmoniums
Circus organs
Swiss barrel organs
George Eastman House—Rochester
Photographic items
West Point Museum—United States Military Academy
Weapons
Flags
Uniforms
Terminal Barber Shop—Radio City, New York City
Tonsorial exhibit
1,200 shaving mugs
63 basins
Smith's Clove Museum—Monroe
Early craft items
Rag carpet
Glass
Pottery
Norcross Greeting Cards—New York City
Valentines
Mary Chess Perfumes—New York City
Perfume bottles

Stony Point Gallery—Stony Point
    Primitives
    Weather vanes
    Decoys
    Garden figures
Suffolk Museum—Stony Brook
    Melville Collection of 300 horse-drawn vehicles, carriages,
        sleds, wagons back to 1695
Shaker Museum—Old Chatham
    Shaker boxes
    Shaker furniture
    Costumes
    Spirit writings
Farmer's Museum—Cooperstown
    Drug items
    Medical items
    Blacksmith tools
    Old printing press and implements
    Country-store items
Corning Glass Center—Corning
    Glass of all periods
Museum of the Home Insurance Company—New York City
    Fire-fighting items
    Helmets
    Buckets
    Trumpets
    Marks
    Prints
    Torches
    Bells
    Axes
    Shields
    Lanterns
Lewyt Corp.—Brooklyn
    Household cleaning implements
Arnold Bakers—Port Chester
    Arnold Collection of Bread Trays (traveling)

Rudolph Wurlitzer Co.—New York City
  Violins
Jewish Museum—New York City
  Ceremonial pieces
  Silver
  Brass
  Ceramics
B. Blumenthal and Company—New York City
  Pearl buttons (prize-winning, 1878)
Bailey Green and Elger, Inc.—New York City
  Buttons—pearl—French

North Carolina

Country Store Terminal of the Tweetsie R. R.—Blowing Rock
  Country-store items

Ohio

Western Reserve Historical Society Museum—Cleveland
  Fans
  Ruby glass
Taft Museum—Cincinnati
  Duncan Phyfe furniture
Cincinnati Art Museum
  W. T. H. Howe Collection of Early American Glass
  William Howard Doane Collection of Musical Instruments
  Arthur Joseph Collection of Meissen
  United States Playing Card Collection of Playing Cards
Telsex Company—Springfield
  Poultry figures
Rookwood Pottery—Mt. Adams, Cincinnati
  Rookwood
First National Bank—Fostoria
  Emerine Collection of mechanical banks
  Mechanical toys
Museum of Art—Toledo
  Glass

D.A.R. Museum—Springfield
Buttons—B. Grace Porter Collection

Oklahoma

Chuck Wagon Café—Atoka
Mechanical music players

Pennsylvania

Philadelphia Museum of Art
Pennsylvania Dutch items—Titus Geesey Collection
Shawls
Textiles
Philadelphia silver
Tucker china
Miniatures
Reading Public Museum and Art Gallery—Reading
Sgraffito pottery
Free Library of Philadelphia
Historical prints
Greeting cards
Trade cards
Post cards
Posters
Hornbooks
Borneman Collection of Fractur
Kate Greenaway Items
Pennsylvania Farm Museum—Landisville
Baskets
Stoves
Lehnware
Musical instruments
Guns
Many other collections of Americana being added as they
are classified
Chester Country Historical Society—West Chester
Tucker china
Valentines

Paper dolls
Dollhouse furniture
Dolls—over 1,000
Quilts
Samplers
Snuffboxes
American Swedish Historical Foundation—Philadelphia
  Jenny Lind items
Hershey Museum—Hershey
  Stiegel glass
Washington Memorial Museum—Valley Forge
  Historic blue Staffordshire
  Silver luster
  Majolica
  Pottery
  Gaudy Dutch
  Washington items
Wedgwood Museum—Merion
  Collection of H. M. Buten
  Jasper
  Basalt
  Creamware
  Caneware
  Redware
  Tortoise
  Salt glaze
Hamilton Watch Co.—Lancaster
  Watches
Stephen Whitman Co., City Line Avenue—Philadelphia
  Samplers
Franklin Institute—Philadelphia
  Frankliniana
Kelly's of Mole Street (Oyster-House)—Philadelphia
  Collection of oyster plates and other marine ceramics
Font Hill—Doylestown
  Moravian pottery

The Bucks County Historical Society, Mercer Museum—Doyles-
town
    Tools of all trades
    Goods and gear up to the machine age
    Implements
Moravian Museum—Lititz
    High-seat Windsors
Alfred University College of Ceramics—Pittsburgh
    Alfred Silverman Glass Collection
    Pittsburgh Glass
    Locke Glass
Johnston's Old Toy Shop Museum—Brandon
    Dolls
    Toys
    Trains
    Chalkware
Gettysburg National Museum
    Military items
    Civil War relics
Fort Hunter Museum—Harrisburg
    Pewter
    Pitchers
    Costumes
    Toys
Historical Society of Berks Co.—Reading
    Pennsylvania iron
    Stove plates
    Firebacks
    Farm implements
    Butter molds
The Book Barn—West Chester
    Country-store collection

Rhode Island

Rhode Island Historical Society—Providence
    Pewter
    Ephemera

Rhode Island furniture
Old Slater Mill—Pawtucket
Spinning and weaving items
Faunce Art Gallery—Providence
Abby Aldrich Rockefeller Collection of Bird and Flower
Prints
Carrington House—Providence
Chinese and French wallpapers

Tennessee

American Egyptian Hall—Nashville
Collection of magic memorabilia

Vermont

Bennington Historical Museum and Art Gallery—Bennington
Bennington pottery
Parian
Flint enamel
Glass
Costumes
Uniforms
Flags
Shelburne Museum—Shelburne, South of Burlington
Rugs
Quilts
Bandboxes
Toys
Silhouettes
Daguerreotypes
Tobies
Fireboards
Fire buckets
Signs
Eagles
Ships' figureheads
Weather vanes
Tools

Decoys
Stencils
Needlework pictures
Circus items
Dolls
Pewter
Glass
Ceramics
Country-store items
Hats
Miniature furniture
Doll Museum—Thetford
Dolls
Green Mountain Inn—Stowe
Whips

Virginia

Mariner's Museum—Newport News
Ship models
Maritime items
Valentine Museum—Richmond
Half-'n-Half Pipe Collection
Costume accessories—one of the finest
Jewelry
Fans
Parasols
Purses
Virginia Museum of Fine Arts—Richmond
Lillian Thomas Pratt Collection of Imperial Fabergé Easter
Eggs
Stabler-Leadbeater Apothecary Shop—Alexandria
Apothecary items (this shop restored is one of the better
known of thirty-eight scattered throughout the country)
Abby Aldrich Rockefeller Folk Art Collection—Williamsburg
Primitive paintings
Needlework
Figures

West Virginia

Ogleby Institute—Wheeling
    Wheeling glass
    Jewelry
    Pewter

Washington

Seattle Historical Museum—Seattle
    600 pieces of American glass
Seattle Art Museum—Seattle
    300 cup plates

Wisconsin

Neville Public Museum—Green Bay
    David Belasco Collection of Victoriana
    Fans
    Laces
    Costumes and accessories
    Musical instruments
State Historical Society—Madison
    Pauline pottery
Milwaukee County Historical Society Museum—Milwaukee
    Old beer bottles
The John Nelson Bergstrom Art Center and Museum—Neenah
    Bergstrom Collection of Paperweights

Hawaii

Bernice P. Bishop Museum—Honolulu
    Souvenir spoons

District of Columbia

Smithsonian Institution—Washington
    Bristol-Myers Collection of Drug Jars
    Photographic items

11.

END OF THE LINE

WHAT is the ultimate fate of the collection you have so arduously pursued for many years, upon which you have spent a lot of time and money? Does it wither away, unhonored and unsung? Has it been forgotten during times of stress and become buried deep with other mementoes of the past? Have you gotten tired of it and tucked it away casually as just so many dust catchers? If so, it is a tragedy. Any collection of worth should have a destination. And this should be determined almost from the beginning even though it seems far, far away. So many unlooked-for things can happen in even a few short years, money can give out unexpectedly, illness strike, old age creep up, you may have to move to smaller quarters, all things that will affect the fate of the material things you possess and put a stop to acquiring more.

On the chapter on investment this phase of collecting antiques has been partly answered. Maybe you have intended cashing in on them from the beginning when the time was right. And now that time has come. You are ready to part with them. How are you going to go about this business of selling them? In the case of a large and important collection the best course is to give it to a professional auctioneer to put up for sale. However, he is not apt to bother with anything that will not net him a good profit. If he can work your collection in with another sale, he might be able to take your nice collection of one hundred and fifty pieces of luster. It will be up to him to decide if the time is right for selling. Consequently it is very important that you should know your auctioneer and his reputation. This takes some doing. If the auctioneer has been in business a long time and is known to attract good buying crowds, you will probably be in good hands. A way to find out is to go to several of his sales and listen to what is being said around you.

But suppose you can't get an antique auctioneer to handle your collection? There are still the big-city auction houses to consider. Again you run the risk of selling at the wrong time, of insufficient advertising, and so on. You also come up against the problem of price. You can't call off the sale if the day is bad or the crowd thin. Except for well-advertised and notorious collections the auction houses are looked upon more as a means of getting rid of surplus possessions or of quick settling of estates. People go looking for bargains.

A man I know is facing this problem right now. He has inherited a fine collection of old silver pieces numbering several hundreds among which are some good English and American pieces but also quite a bit of less valuable continental silver. He has had the collection appraised and he knows what it should bring when he sells. He has decided against an auction for several reasons, one the commission to be paid, two because he doubts that it will bring the right prices if sold at auction. He may be right. And so he has elected to do the selling himself to dealers and collectors piece by piece. It is going to take time and work but he does not seem to mind. Maybe when he has sold off the best pieces he will let the rest go at auction.

This brings up another query: is it better to sell as an entire collection or piece by piece? Again that will depend upon many things. If you can find a buyer for the collection as a whole, and many times you can among dealers who will take it on, it will save you a lot of worry and work. You may have to make some price concession because of that. But as a rule collections are better broken up for selling. Dealers may find that it is better for the market generally to let the pieces come up for sale gradually. Dumping a large collection on the counter is apt to lower the price—for a time at least. Again it depends upon the popularity of what you have to sell. Dealers are quick to sense any falling off of interest in certain things. They may advise you to hold on for a while, or to sell gradually.

One way to find out for yourself is to send up a trial balloon in an ad, enumerating the pieces in the collection, offering to sell it in whole or in part. Or you can try selling it as a whole to a museum. Many museums do not buy collections, or only at times. They wait to have them donated to them. On the other hand, if there is something quite special that they may want and they are in funds you may be able to do business with them.

If you are going to take on the sale of your pieces yourself you will have to let the world of other collectors know about it. You can do it by word of mouth, through friends, other collectors you know, through an association if you belong to one, through dealers, and so on. Or you can advertise it in local papers, in journals of interested societies, in the pages of the magazines devoted to antiques and hobbies. You should be ready with an inventory, full details on the prices which you feel are right in relation to the current market. Have these lists mimeographed so they may be distributed easily. If you feel you are going to do a lot of this selling by mail, have some pictures taken good enough to show the details of the pieces.

You may decide to do the selling by contact, piece by piece, in your home or the shop of a friend. Or you can limit the selling to a three-day sale, getting out notices to all dealers in your area and to other interested collectors. You are doing the same thing on a small scale that the auctioneer does, only your prices should be specified and stable—not determined by bidding. You will have to decide whether you are going to give the buying dealers a discount or whether you will keep it on a strictly retail basis. If the latter, it had better be so stated with the announcement. It will all depend upon what you feel your prices will attract or how fast you want to get rid of your pieces.

There is another consideration if you are in no great hurry to realize on your collection and that is to give it to a dealer on a consignment basis. In this way it is not all sold at once and a dealer who might not be able to put up the cash for the collection in its entirety would be glad to display it in his shop with a mark up sufficient to take care of his 20 per cent commission. You should settle on the prices between you, and they should not be changed without your consent. Or there is the possibility of a buyer buying part of your collection and keeping the rest on a consignment basis.

No matter how you plan to sell it, it is going to cost you money, and you better make up your mind to that. You may hit the top of the market and you may not, but if your investment has been seasoning for some years you should come out with a good profit. One thing, keep a careful record of expenses involved with this selling. These can come off the profit before you declare it on your income tax.

Maybe you don't want to sell your entire collection, only a part of it. All collections are apt to get topheavy over the years. There comes a point of saturation when they become hard to store, a burden to take care of. You have made mistakes in buying, paying too much for some pieces, getting items that were good fillers but not good enough to keep after you have found the better pieces. You go about selling off in the same ways as suggested above only you don't have so much to dispose of. You may find it advantageous to take them to another part of the country for sale. You may have to do quite a bit of shopping around for good prices, because dealers cannot give you top retail prices or how would they make a profit? This whole business of buying and selling antiques is a great game. It requires not only a lot of knowledge but an ability to keep dollar values in your head, to juggle and average up, a loss here, a profit there. So if you have no head for business, you had better let someone else do it for you even if you have to pay for the service.

Perhaps you have no intention of selling. You have decided to give your collection away. It has served its purpose. It has given you much pleasure over the years, and after all you can't take it with you. If so, why not give it where it will be appreciated most? Gifts from your collection are wonderful ways of repaying old favors and debts, sealing old friendships, remembering the people you love while you are alive, and enjoying their joy in your generosity. It often saves a lot of squabbling after you are gone. One woman has labeled all her best pieces for distribution after her death. The recipients know what they are going to get and are properly grateful the while she holds on to her treasures and enjoys them to the end. Each piece has a label telling what it is, date and place of origin (if possible), date it came into her possession, who is to have it, and any other interesting data about it. In fact, it is a good idea to so label any antique piece that you give away.

You may feel that the place for your collection is in a museum where it will be of benefit to other collectors or students. How often you have heard an older person say, "I don't know what to do with my collection of snuffboxes. My children aren't interested in old things." But don't act too quickly. It might be wise to give your family the choice of keeping them or giving them to some museum. The tastes of young people change quickly. Now, believe it or not, every museum does not want many of the things that are left to it. They may have similar things or no room in which to store them. Or they may not be interested in the kind of thing you are aiming to give them. Consequently, if you are thinking seriously of disposing of your collection this way it might be a good idea to inquire and find out where your collection would be welcome. You will probably prefer giving it to some place close to home, your local historical society perhaps, if it comprises objects of local interest. But do go into it carefully with the curator before you do anything definite about it. If he is not interested, he may be able to tell you where it would be acceptable.

As a rule museums prefer outright gifts to loans. They do not want strings to these borrowed collections, to be told when and where to exhibit them, or run the risk of having the heirs change their minds about letting the museum have them for any length of time.

There is a big advantage in giving your collection to a museum or other charitable institution during your lifetime.

You can take it off your income tax. In the deduction for charities and donations you can list the collection at the "fair market value" of the date it is donated. This will mean an appraisal, not by the museum but by a recognized appraiser unless such an appraisal has been made very recently. Now in this deduction, which comes under contributions on the itemized deduction page of your income-tax form, you are entitled to claim not more than 20 per cent of your adjusted gross income for the taxable year, or 30 per cent under certain circumstances which might include churches, tax-exempt educational institutions, tax-exempt hospitals, and certain medical-research organizations. So the first thing to establish is whether the museum or other organization of your choice comes under the deductible clause or not—most museums do —and whether it might fall in the 20 per cent or 30 per cent bracket. Then you must determine whether the whole collection falls within the limit of deduction allowed for one year. If it is too large, you can usually make it a loan, writing off a deduction for part of it as a contribution each year until the whole thing is cleared off.

As a matter of fact, you don't actually have to give up possession of your collection during your lifetime if you *give* it to the institution with their permission for you to keep it until you die. You can still take the tax deduction or deductions in this period.

And so your collection, while not bringing in a cash profit as an investment, can do two things, ease up on the income-tax figure and insure that others coming after you will have the enjoyment of it. There is another angle to this. Your collection might be proving a loss. Instead of selling it and taking the loss on your income tax as a capital loss, it might pay you to give it away and claim the deduction instead. Figure it out to your best advantage.

Of course this deduction applies only to institutions, not individuals. There is another way of sharing your collection with the public by establishing a small museum of your own. This is a nice thing to do. Of course the collection must be big enough and important enough to be worth showing. It does not destroy the investment value of your pieces, they can still be sold or given away later, but in this way the owner can be enjoying them while he shares them.

You may decide to do nothing about your collection, just hold on and let those who come after you worry about it. You may feel the few things you have collected will not make a lot of difference in settling your estate for inheritance-tax purposes. But they might possibly tip the scale over the minimum established by Uncle Sam or the state. Your heirs can handle the collection in several ways. It will have to be appraised as of the time of your death. Then it can be divided, if necessary, according to the terms of your will. Certainly if there is going to be any ill will engendered by its disposal, it would be better to do the dividing yourself before you pass on or with a schedule attached to your will so that the heirs get the pieces you want them to have. Moreover, some of the heirs may want to sell and get their share of the cash rather than the pieces, thus forcing an interested heir to have to buy in the collection if he wants it. Squabbling over Great-aunt Emily's silver tea service or Uncle Dudley's grandfather's clock has ended in more family feuds than corner lots in a boom-development area. So to be safe do the dividing before you go, give your possessions where you want them to go but retain them for the duration of your lifetime. You can give away as much as $3,000 of your estate a year, and many people use this loophole to avoid big inheritance taxes.

So whether you sell off, give away, lend it, or leave it to your family it should reach others who will appreciate it. Just don't forget it and neglect it until it gets lost, broken, or deteriorates. The end of the line for any good collection should be another antique lover's cupboard, not the dark corners of a junk shop.

Appendix A

ASSOCIATIONS

It has been estimated that there are almost five hundred national organizations and associations in this country covering various interests 20 per cent of which relate to antiques or antiquities in some way. For the purpose of this book, useful information for the beginning collector, here are some of the more important associations where he can come in contact with others interested in his hobby:

The Questers
> Box 127, Ambler, Pa.
> This is an association for anyone interested in antiques generally as well as for collectors. It has grown to national dimension with 102 chapters in 18 states coast to coast (as of spring 1959), some of which are husband-and-wife affairs.

Coverlet Guild
> Mrs. Harold S. Sanke
> R.D. #2, Wooded Shores
> Wonder Lake, Ill.

Wedgwood Club
> Mrs. Charles Goreley,
> Gore Lea, Weston 95, Mass.

The Wedgwood Society
 Mr. Harry M. Buten
 Buten Wedgwood Museum
 246 North Bowman Avenue
 Merion, Pa.

American Bell Association
 R.F.D. #1
 Tarentum, Pa.

Old Lacers
 Mrs. Louise Leonberger
 88 Juanita Way
 San Francisco 27, Cal.

National Button Society
 Lillian Albert Smith
 Hightstown, N. J.

United Federation of Doll Clubs
 Mrs. Rudolf Seibert
 109 Sandringham Street
 Rochester 10, N. Y.

International Music Box Society
 Mrs. Clarence W. Fabel
 4301 Forest Manor Avenue
 Indianapolis 18, Ind.

National Society of Powder Horn and Flask Collectors
 Mr. C. Stanley Jacob
 202 West 8th Street
 Plainfield, N. J.

National Early American Glass Club
 Mrs. John B. Hitchins
 31 Norwood Street
 Sharon, Mass.

Paperweight Collectors' Association
  Mr. Paul Jokelson
  55 West 42nd Street
  New York 36, N. Y.

National Association of Watch and Clock Collectors
  Mr. George E. Shaw
  R. D. #2
  Victory Heights
  Franklin, Pa.

Standard Gauge Association Inc. (Toy Trains)
  107 Park Avenue
  Harrison, N. Y.

Pewter Collectors' Club of America
  Mr. Thomas D. Williams
  Litchfield, Conn.

American Gramophone Society (for the preservation of
  Master Records)
  1226 Montgomery Avenue
  Narberth, Pa.

The Civil War Round Table
  c/o Army and Navy Club
  1627 Eye Street N. W.
  Washington, D. C.

American Arms Collectors' Association, Inc.
  John H. Wetzelberger
  1101 Hampton Garth
  Towson 4, Md.

Early American Industries
  Joseph W. Rake
  161 Broadway
  Newburg, N. Y.

Playing Card Collectors' Ass'n., Inc.
  Mrs. Walter Boeyer
  3869 North 84th Street
  Milwaukee, Wis.

Added to these, of course, are many local clubs which it should not be too hard for the collector to trace in his own area. A letter to any of the above will probably bring details of chapters throughout the country and procedure for becoming affiliated with them. The addresses given are as permanent as possible taking into consideration change of officers over the years.

Appendix B

GUIDE TO 1,000 ITEMS
TO COLLECT

As explained in Chapter 3, many items listed here are mentioned more than once because they fall under several categories. Though defined for easier identification wherever necessary it is suggested that you follow up your choice with some preliminary study through books, magazines, and visits to museums and shops, so that you may recognize what you are about to collect. The asterisks indicate the 200 most sought-after collectibles.

1. *Furniture*

Stools—ranging from small primitive wooden ones through the period pieces to Victorian, including hassocks and piano stools

Lap desks—these small writing cases were made to rest upon the knees, table or stand. Really a portable desk. Popular for traveling. Made in food of all kinds, also papier-mâché.

Small chests—includes blanket chests, dowry chests, small trunks and traveling boxes, money and document boxes

Small cabinets—hanging wall cabinets of all kinds, as well as cabinets of drawers used in apothecary shops, old stores, doctor's offices, etc.

Stands—small occasional tables, sewing stands, bed tables, candle stands, wig stands, and washstands

Benches—from the primitive backless wooden porch bench or bench for washtubs to the church pew, upholstered fireside bench, window bench, piano bench, and the Windsor and painted settees

*Miniature or children's pieces—not toys, but small-sized replicas of furniture like chairs, chests, tables, etc.

Spice cabinets—from the finest period pieces with drawers and compartments, feet, and an outer door (often called Chester County pieces in Pennsylvania where many were made) to the primitive wooden tier of drawers for kitchen use

Canterburies and music stands—now copied for magazine stands with upright compartments. Fine pieces for holding portfolios, prints, maps, etc.

What-nots—Victorian sets of open shelves for displaying bric-a-brac or curios. Wall type or corner type, shelves often graduated in width. Seen most often in spool turning

2. *Silver*

Sterling silver—area for beginning collectors from 1825 to 1900. The name of sterling, however, was not generally used on American silver until after 1860. Content .925 silver

Coin silver—the name given to early American silver, which was originally made from silver coins melted down as silver was not successfully mined in the United States until the mid-1800's. After 1830 the word *coin, pure coin, dollar,* or the initials *C or D* was stamped on coin silver to indicate that it was of the same content as U.S. mint silver used in coins, not that it was made from melted coins. Content .900 silver

Sheffield—a process of welding two layers of silver over a filling of copper. Perfected in England in 1742. No Sheffield was made in America. Practically everything made in silver was also made in Sheffield plate except flat silver. The list includes

　　Trays
　　Candlesticks

Candelabra

Buckets

Pitchers

Epergnes—branched centerpieces for fruit and flowers

Coffee and tea urns

Sugars—with colored glass bowls

Salts—with colored glass inserts

Inkstands

Tea sets

Cake and fruit baskets

Tureens

Dish crosses—stands for hot dishes

Wine coolers

Cruet stands—for bottles, jars, etc.

Wirework pieces—wholly or partly made of silver over copper wire

*Electroplated silver—not to be confused with Sheffield—a galvanic process of electroplating a silver coating on a white metal base or one of britannia. Dates in this country from about 1850. It was the popular table silver for those who could not afford sterling—still is. Besides the usual pieces of tea sets, coffeepots, etc., are to be found cake baskets, pudding dishes, castor stands, pickle jars, cracker jars (both with glass), butter dishes, spoon holders, goblets, egg-cup stands, and so on

Flat table pieces, sterling or plated—a rewarding field to explore for the beginner. Would include besides place settings

Berry spoons

Condiment spoons

Stuffing spoons

Pie servers

Cheese servers

Fish servers

Ladles

Small serving forks

Large serving tongs

Sugar tongs—for lump sugar

Sugar cutters—used when sugar came in solid blocks
Grape scissors—for cutting small clusters from the large
bunch
*Napkin rings
Knife rests—for parking the carving set
Open salts
Salt and pepper shakers
Muffineers—shakers for salt or sugar
Marrow spoons—for scooping the marrow from bones
Caddy spoons—for use with tea caddies or containers
Skimmers—for removing tea leaves from the brew
Strainer spoons—for serving watery vegetables or meat
Café Brûlé spoons—for burning brandy over coffee
*Spoons—one of the most popular collectibles. The range is wide,
from such things as Apostle Spoons (old English christening
spoons in sets of twelve, an apostle to each spoon, with the
Master spoon very rare) through novelty spoons such as
Monkey Spoons, Postage Stamp Spoons, Advertising Spoons,
etc., through many patterns old and new including Rattail
(with pointed reinforcement on back of bowl), Coffin Lid
(from shape of handle, often memorially inscribed), Fiddle
Shape, Shovel, Shell, and so on
*Souvenir spoons—a large and popular area to specialize in with
many classifications based on dates, localities, events, per-
sonages, etc. Still not expensive
Children's mugs
Tea caddies—for storing the tea leaves. Used on the tea table
Candlesticks
Inkstands
Snuffers and snuffer trays—for putting out candle flames
Lamps
Wine labels—to hang on the decanters
Dresser sets
Toilet articles
Buckles
Buttons
Toys, rattles, etc.

*Soapboxes—for traveling

Pieces made by certain makers, or certain localities—Rogers, Reed and Barton, Meriden, Baltimore silver, Philadelphia silver, etc.

3. Glass

*Lacy glass—early pressed glass made first at Sandwich, Cape Cod, Massachusetts, in 1825. Of more interest to advanced collector, though the beginner might choose to pursue the cup plates both Sandwich and Midwestern. Beware of reproductions

*Pressed glass—a tremendous classification running from the early lacy glass of 1840 up to the late patterns of the 1890's. Hundreds of patterns and variants of the pattern glass

Opaque glass—not transparent

    *Milk white—opaque white. Also blue, green, yellow, and rare pink

    *Marbled often called slag—purple, yellow, and brown with marble-like streaks of darker color

    Caramel—deep creamy tan

    Camphor—cloudy like gum camphor

    Clam broth—cloudy white

    Custard—cream-colored, made in West Virginia about 1898

    Opaline—glass with a milky iridescence

*Colored glass

    Blue—cornflower, aquamarine, sapphire, cobalt

    Green—bottle, apple, olive, jade, peacock

    Yellow—vaseline, amber, canary, citron, olive

    Red—cranberry, ruby, pigeon's blood

    Amethyst—violet, purple, magenta

    Black— (deep olive, amethyst or amber)

    Opalescent—blue opalescent, yellow opalescent

*Art glass—late nineteenth-century fancy glass, blown, blown-molded, or pressed. Most of this is expensive, but available

    Agata—shading white to rose, mottled

    Amberina—clear glass running clear amber to ruby

    Aurene—gold iridescent, usually marked or labeled

Burmese—shading from soft canary yellow to rose pink—not clear

Cameo-Gallé—a cased glass (with contrasting colored lining) pattern cut from the overlay

Nicholas Lutz—striped or threaded Venetian type, made by a Frenchman at Boston and Sandwich Co. Sometimes marked

Kew Blas—opal or milk glass flashed or stained with color and coated with clear glass. Usually marked

Mother-of-Pearl—a type of satin glass (glass treated with acid vapor to give it a satinlike finish)

Peachblow—made to resemble Chinese porcelain—usually shading from white to rose with milk white under layer. Glossy or acid finish

Pomona—with two surfaces, one etched in pebbled effect, the other of flashed or tinted glass. Occasionally patterned

Rubina—shading from clear to ruby—sometimes frosted

Rubina Verde—shading from yellow-green to cranberry

Satin—opal or milk-white base molded in quilted, circular, or square depressions with a transparent coating. In many colors, mostly pink and blue

Vasa Murrhina—brilliant flecks of mica or other metals

Thomas Webb—product of an English maker of satin and other art glass

Iridescent

Tiffany—called Favrile by maker, Louis Tiffany. Gold iridescent or lustered glass usually marked

Quezal—much like Tiffany. An overlay glass, the overlay drawn into various designs or shapes, notably the peacock eye

Taffeta or Carnival—cheap imitation of better iridescent varieties, mostly orange and purple

Cut and engraved glass—deep and shallow cutting done by the same process with a wheel. Etched glass is done with acid biting through a pattern cut in a coating of asphaltum. The early period takes in the first glassmakers such as Stiegel,

Amelung, et al. as well as English and Irish imports. Of more interest to beginners are

American Middle Period—1830–65
Pittsburgh
Sandwich
New England Glass Co.
Mt. Washington
Dorflinger's
Dummer
Unidentified pieces.

*American Brilliant Period—1880–1905
As much of this glass and the preceding group was not marked, it requires study to identify it. Some makers, such as Libbey and Hawkes, cut their marking on the base of the piece. Others used paper labels.
Libbey—Ohio
Pairpont—New Bedford, Massachusetts
Gillinder—Philadelphia
Dorflinger—White Mills, Pennsylvania
Corning—New York
Fry—Rochester, New York
Heisey
Unmarked and later pieces not so desirable.

Millefiori—meaning 1,000 flowers. Effect gained by cutting across varicolored glass rods or canes. Used for paperweights, vases, cruets, etc.

Silver Inlay—glass with decorations of silver deposit

Mercury—flashed or coated inside with mercury to look like silver

*Mary Gregory—clear and colored glass decorated with painted or enameled figures in white of children, women, flowers, etc., named for the artist at the Boston and Sandwich factory

*End-of-Day—mottled and varicolored. Supposedly made by workmen of leftovers of colored glass

United States Coin—made only for five months in 1892. Banned by the Treasury as counterfeit because it used real coins for the molds. Rare and expensive

Columbian Coin—not to be confused with United States Coin—
the decorations are not real coins, only medallions. Much
less expensive

Bohemian—originally made in Bohemia, Czechoslovakia. A fine
flashed (coated) colored glass usually ruby with cut or etched
pattern of clear or frosted glass. English, Germans, and Swiss
made imitations. Imported from 1825 on. Available pieces
from 1875 to 1900 period. Still being made

Baccarat—French glass made in town of the same name—many
kinds of glass as well as paperweights. Still made. Sometimes
marked

Lalique—a French glass in vogue from 1905 to 1930. Pressed,
blown, frosted, and cut

Vallerystahl—from Lorraine, France. Often confused with American milk glass

*American Bristol—not to be confused with English Bristol. A
frosted glass with painted and gold decoration

American Nailsea-type—two-toned glass with white and colored
swirls

*Lesser-known types of American glass, such as Redford, Findlay,
Wheeling, Wavecrest, etc., offer collectors many interesting
by-paths to explore, especially if the glass was made locally.

Classified by individual pieces

　*Covered animal dishes—hens, cats, rabbits, swans, etc.,
　　mostly in white and colored milk glass. Sometimes in
　　frosted glass

　Atomizers

　Balls

　　Witch balls—originally hung in windows as a protection
　　　against witches

　　Seine—used to float seines instead of corks

　　Jar covers—used to fit in the opening of a jar or bottle
　　　instead of a cover or cork

　　*Marbles—many old ones were of colored and striped
　　　glass—sulphides were of glass with small silvered
　　　figure encased in center

Target balls—for trapshooting. Bogardus balls named
for the champion much sought after. Balls are colored, usually blue or amber, with a hole through
which they could be filled with feathers, confetti,
smoke, etc. Some were corrugated to keep bullet
from glancing off surface

Banks—many penny banks were made of glass in figural
shapes such as animals, houses, Liberty Bell, etc.

Brides' baskets—given as wedding presents in 1880–1900
period. Fancy colored glass in silver metal basket

Beer glasses—beer or ale glasses were made in many of the
pressed-glass patterns, even the earlier ones. As hollow
stems are being made illegal in many places, look for
these for future interest

Birdcage dishes—for seed and water. Often milk glass. Some
blown

Bobêches—the disks used on top of the candle socket to catch
the wax

Bottles

Wine bottles—look for all old bottles up to 1875, when
form became about the same as current bottles.
Some novelty bottles of the present are worth saving

Demijohns—word is a corruption of French *dame-
jeanne*. A bottle for wine or spirits holding from
one to ten gallons enclosed in wickerwork. Also
called a carboy

Apothecary—labeled drug bottles clear or blue. Occasionally amber

Barber—for tonic and bay rum. Often personalized with
name of owner. Many examples of fine glass including overlay and Bohemian

Bellows—shaped like a bellows. Very fancy, with applied
decoration and swirled color

Blacking—for shoe blacking. Early bottles were square
and blown

*Bitters—more than 500 known impressed bottles with
trade names of a medicine that was mostly alcohol

Chestnut—round, flat bottle in chestnut shape called
   Ludlow bottle, a species of carboy from miniature
   to demijohn size
Cologne or bureau bottles—usually in pairs
*Figural or character bottles—of many shapes and sizes
   and made for many purposes, liquor, perfume,
   medicine. Novelty bottles of pre- and post-Civil War
   period, whimsical early "packaging." More than
   700 have been listed. Most desirable are the Moses,
   George Washington bust, Santa Claus, to name a
   few
Character
      Human figures
      Portrait busts
Animal
      Fish and reptiles
      Shells
      Birds
Objects
      Fruits
      Vegetables
      Boots and shoes
      Watches, clocks, buildings, revolvers, dice, vio-
      lin, pretzel, barrel, and so on
Gemels—twin bottles fused together with two necks
   bending in opposite directions
Half bottles—like a whole bottle cut in half
Ink
Medicine
Nursing
*Perfume—from early Stiegel and South Jersey seahorse
   to 1900 cut glass
Pickle—including the paneled "cathedral" bottle
Saddle—made flat to slip in a saddlebag
Scent and smelling salts
Soda pop
Snuff

Vinegar

Whisky

Bread trays

Bull's-eye glass—convex panes of window glass with large pontil mark in center—translucent, but not transparent

Candlesticks

Candy or sweetmeat jars

*Candy containers—guns, locomotives, suitcases, etc., once filled with penny candy

Canes

Carafes—water bottles

Castor bottles and castor stands—for vinegar, oil, catsup

Celery vases

Christmas-tree lights—colored glass cups to hold candles

Compotes, covered and uncovered

Creamers

*Cruets

Custard glasses

Decanters

Egg Cups

Epergnes

Eye cups—for eye wash. Many colors

Finger bowls

*Flasks a large collecting area from 1800 to 1875

Historical

Commemorative

Masonic

Portrait

Pictorial

Shape or form

Flip glasses—large tumbler for a drink called flip

Goblets

*Hats

Honey dishes

Inkwells

*Jars

Apothecary—window—leech—sponge

Candy store—from old stores. With glass or japanned tin tops
Mason—early canning jars
Other preserving jars
Jelly glasses—early ones were like large tumblers
Jugs
Knobs
    Door—cut glass or striped like paperweights
    Furniture—Sandwich and others. Plain and opalescent
    Mirror—to support hanging mirror on lower corners
    Newel post—spheres and other shapes to top the newel post
        of stairs
Lamp bases—in all the pressed and colored varieties
Match holders
Miniature objects—doll dishes, etc.
Muffineers
Mugs
Mustard pots
*Paperweights
    French—Baccarat, St. Louis, Clichy, very expensive and
        beyond average beginner's scope
    Sandwich—from Sandwich Glass Co., Massachusetts
    Milville—from New Jersey glass factory. Outstanding is the
        Milville Rose. Even the reproduction is now valuable
    Gilliland—Brooklyn
    By lesser known American makers
    Fruit
    Figural—frog, Liberty Bell, etc.
    Motto
    Souvenir
Peg lamps—small oil-well lamps with a stopper to fit into a
    candlestick
Pickle dishes and jars
Pitchers
Plates
Platters
Potpourri jars—for spiced rose petals or other dried flowers
*Powder jars—for the bureau

Prisms—crystal drops for lamps, candelabra, or chandeliers

Punch cups

Rolling pins—sometimes whimsical and often useful

*Rose bowls—a round bowl with small opening for holding roses

Salesmen's samples—toy size. Mostly table pieces in pressed-glass patterns

*Salt dips—open salts. In many varieties of glass from Stiegel down to late cut glass. Clear and colored. Some in whimsical shapes

Sauce dishes—plain and footed

Spill holders—vases to hold tapers made of twisted paper called spills for lighting fires

Spoon holder—a vase for holding extra tablespoons or teaspoons

Shaving-paper vases—part of the barbershop equipment. Often matched the barber bottles

*Shoes, slippers, boots, skates—whimsical shapes for match or toothpick holders, or often just for ornament

Smoke bells—flower-like disks or cups to hang over a lamp, chandelier, or candelabrum to prevent smoke from blackening ceiling

*Souvenir pieces—of red and clear or all-red glass or white and gold called Koral, having the name of a resort and the date or the name of the recipient

Sugar bowls

*Syrup jugs

Tea-caddy canisters—the glass jars that fit inside the tea caddy

*Toothpick holders

*Tumblers in colored glass—a popular collectible

Transparencies and lithophanes—to hang in windows or used in various ways where light could show through. There were painted ones and black-and-white lithophanes like old prints with cast intaglio designs to produce a picture of light and shade when held to the light. Many objects were made of them, shields for candle sconces, lampshades, bottoms of beer steins, etc.

Vases

Vigil lights—cups to hold a thick candle for a night light or
altar light

Water sets—pitcher and tumblers often on a matching tray

Whisky glasses

Wig stands—tall stands like pyramids resembling paperweights

Window glass

Panes from old windows that show bubbles or irregularities

Sun-amethyst panes from windows that have been purpled
by sunlight

Motifs from old church windows

Pressed-glass panels, frosted or colored, from old doorways

Wineglasses

Whimseys—amusing odds and ends used on what-nots, hats, shoes,
canes, hatchets, gypsy kettles, canoes, pipes, chains, canes, etc.

4. *China and Pottery*

American

Redware pottery—primitive ware of red clay. Glazed only on the
inside of pieces

*Slipware—designs applied on cream or brown base with con-
trasting soft slip like cake icing

*Sgraffito—designs scratched through a slip casing to show con-
trasting base

Tucker china—a hard bone porcelain made in Philadelphia from
1825–37. Resembled French china

Staffordshire imports—much English china of the early 1800's was
made to export to America by the various potters of Staffordshire, the center of English pottery making

Classified according to makers:

Stevenson

Clews

Ridgway

Meakin

Stubbs

Tams

Adams

Jackson

Mayor

Rogers

Enoch Wood

Green

Mellor, Venables and Co.

Many lesser known, such as Godwin, Ellsmore, Foster, etc.

Historic Blue—Early American scenes and personages in the early 1800's. Light blue and dark blue, color often flowing

*Later American scenes—in blue and other colors up to 1850–60

Salt glaze—a hard-glaze pottery made by throwing salt into the kiln. Usually white, sometimes decorated

Dr. Syntax plates—comic pictures of the fictional character created by William Combe

*Flow Blue—followed the Historic Blue, color allowed to flow into background. Oriental patterns such as Scinde, Formosa, Chapoo, Manila, Corean, etc. Also Flow Brown

Liverpool pitchers—pitchers of creamware with transfer-printed pictures of historical scenes and personages

Gaudy Dutch—a brightly colored painted china using the Imari motifs, exported to America and supposedly liked by the Pennsylvania Dutch. Expensive

*Gaudy Welch—similar, designs not so definite, always shows a touch of luster. Not quite so expensive

Spatter—china decorated with spatter designs in color. Peafowl, Schoolhouse, Star, Deer, Beehive, Tulip, Windmill, Cannon, Sailboat are some of the patterns

Strawberry—early soft paste in same category with Gaudy Dutch and Spatterware. Strawberry decoration

Roseware—early rose-decorated china. Includes the Adams Rose made 1820–40 and the King's Rose of the same period and exported to Pennsylvania with the Gaudy Dutch

*Mocha—a creamware decorated with seaweed or tree silhouettes and other dipped brush patterns with bands of

black, white, or colors on backgrounds of tan, terra cotta, and blue. Sometimes called Banded Creamware

Queen's Ware or Creamware—begun by Wedgwood but widely copied. A creamy ware with a high glaze. Much of it pierced or of basket weave

*Luster—very popular import from England in the early 1800's. America made no luster. A china partly or entirely covered with a metallic film. Copper produced *copper luster,* platinum gave a *silver* effect, gold came out *pink* or *purple.* There were pearly effects, too. Many Staffordshire potters made it, but the most important are Sunderland and Wedgwood

*Ironstone—one of the most rewarding classifications for the beginning collector. This is the sturdy ware first put out by Miles Mason in 1813. It replaced earthenware for popular use, was more practical than porcelain. It will be found marked quite often with maker's name and names like Stoneware, Granite, Semi-Porcelain. Minnie Watson Kamm reports almost two hundred patterns of English origin, many of which were reproduced over here. Only a few of the more popular patterns can be listed here.

> Willow
> Tea Leaf
> Wheat
> Washington Vase
> Spode's Towers—early and late
> Moss Rose
> Indian Tree
> Blanket Stitch
> Canton
> Bamboo
> Lake of Como
> White undecorated
> > Davenport Fig

Cable

Ceres

*Haviland

A French china from Limoges imported to this country. Also made in America under firm name. Patterns are usually identified by number. Very popular collectible. Suggest Arlene Schleiger's book for pattern identification

*Meissen Onion—a blue-and-white pattern made in the late 1800's. Reproductions still imported

*Rose Medallion—a Chinese ware having medallions with figures alternating with panels of flowers, birds, and butterflies

Noritake—Japanese, marked. Made first in 1904. Over 100 patterns (early pieces hand painted)

Danish Christmas plates—blue-and-white porcelain. A different series every year for over fifty years

Royal Bayreuth 1875–1900, German

Tapestry—a desirable pattern

Figure pieces like apples, tomatoes, etc.

Royal Bonn—German. Most available are Victorian pieces

Royal Doulton—English, still made. Most available dates from 1890

Rudelstadt—German, late nineteenth-century pieces available for beginning collectors

Royal Vienna (beehive mark)—Meissen-type

Carlsbad—Austrian. Widely imported after 1891

*Late Adams Rose—only half as costly as the early ware (1820–40)

*1924 English Chelsea—made from old molds found in the Spode-Copeland works

Majolica—an old ware, tin-enameled, originating in Spain. Called faïence in Italy and France

English

*American

Phoenixville—Etruscan, one of the best known from the Pennsylvania town by Griffen Smith and Hill up to 1892

Bennett—Baltimore, in the 1850's

Bisque—an unglazed ware, used widely for figures and vases
  French—Very fine. Made at Sèvres and Vincennes
  English—Made at Derby
  American—inferior to imported. Victorian period
*Parian—a ware, mostly unglazed, that looked like marble
  Bennington—best known of high quality
  Other makers—widely produced throughout the country,
    some rather tawdry
*Later American wares
  Dedham—made in Chelsea, Massachusetts, 1860 on. Crackle
    ware and animal patterns are characteristic
  Buffalo Pottery—established in early 1900's. Known for jugs,
    mugs, and commemorative plates
  Pattern dinner sets
*Rookwood 1880–1900—Cincinnati, Ohio. Underglaze decoration
  on soft yellow or brown background. Still made
Hand painted—includes not only the china painted at home in
  the late 1800's but commercial hand-painted ware, much of
  it imported from Germany, France, and Japan. Much of it
  marked. Done on fine china like Limoges. Hand painting is
  done *over* the glaze and is often painted over a transfer de-
  sign
Stoneware
  Bennington—highly prized Vermont product beginning with
    the Norton and Fenton firm in 1843. Noted for hound-
    handled pitchers in Rockingham ware. Made articles of
    all kinds
  Trenton—New Jersey potteries of the mid-1800's, Rocking-
    ham, white and yellow stoneware
  Strasburg, Va.—salt-glazed stoneware made by Solomon and
    Samuel Bell
  *Rockingham—not to be confused with English china of that
    name. A brown glazed ware made by many American
    firms
*Spongeware—a grayish ware daubed in blue
  White earthenware—kitchenware, bowls, molds, etc.
  Yellow earthenware—kitchenware, bowls, molds, etc.

Scoddle—Bennington and others. Also known as *scroddle*. A
variegated stoneware that looks like marble cake
Flint enamel—Bennington and others, somewhat like Rock-
ingham but with other colors infused in the glaze
Classified according to individual pieces
Banks—books, figures, etc.
Bottles—china, pottery, figure, gin, book, Bible, etc.
Bowls
*Bread and milk sets—small bowl and pitcher to match
Bread trays
*Butter chips—small individual butter plates
Butter dishes
Cake plates
Candlesticks
Celery dishes
Cheese dishes—all shapes, round, wedge-shaped, oblong, with
cover for whole or wedge of cheese
*Children's mugs—made for gift or reward purposes, quite
small, transfer printed, luster, Gaudy, etc.
*Children's plates
ABC—with alphabet borders, picture centers
Franklin's maxims—illustrating well-known Franklin
proverbs
Others—children's games, storybook pictures, portraits
of heroes, etc.
Chocolate pots and sets
Coasters
Coffeepots
Compotes
Condiment sets—for mustard, relish, etc.
Cracker or cookie jars—often set in silver frames
Creamers
Crocus pots—with holes through which bulbs could grow
*Cup plates—small plates for holding handleless cups while
hot liquid was drunk from saucer
*Cups and saucers
*Demitasse cups and saucers—go back to late 1800's

Dessert sets

Dinner sets

Dresser sets—matched pieces, tray, bottles, trinket box, etc.

Dresser trays

Egg cups

*Eggs

 Darning

 Nest

 Decorated Easter

*Farmers' cups—giant-size cups and saucers

Fish sets and bone dishes—serving platter with set of crescent-shaped dishes for individual place settings

Ginger jars—Chinese porcelain

Gravy boats

*Grotesqueries—jugs, bottles, flasks, etc., with faces or comic figures

Hair receivers—popular Victorian bureau piece for disposing of hair combings

Hatpin holders—vase with perforated top to hold the long hatpins of the early 1900's

Hot-water jugs

Ice-cream sets—serving bowl and saucedishes to match

Inkwells—made in all kinds of china and pottery, fine and otherwise. A fascinating area to explore

Jam pots

Jardinières and flowerpots

*Leaf dishes—of many wares, notably majolica

*Lids—odd dish lids, collected for matching purposes or for intrinsic beauty

*Molds for pudding and jelly—usually of yellow and white earthenware. Wedgwood made decorated china molds, *very* rare

*Mugs—a wide area for collecting, from early mugs such as the Frog Mug with a realistic frog on the bottom to shock the tipsy drinker and the Puzzle Mug, which had holes through which the potable dripped unless it was held the right way, luster mugs, satyr mugs, Gaudy

wares, and transfer-printed to the Victorian gift and souvenir mugs

*Mustache cups—tea, coffee, and mugs made with a shelf or guard to keep the Victorian gentleman's mustaches out of the liquid

*Oyster plates—with depressions to hold the oysters when served on the half shell. Also clam plates and snail plates

Photo frames

*Pitchers—a rewarding category for the beginning collector, as pitchers were made in all wares, early, late, fine, and not so fine. Notable are the hound-handled pitchers, with the figure of a hound for the handle, apostle pitchers, with twelve panels, an apostle for each panel, and met with in salt-glaze ware; Liverpool pitchers with transfer-printed pictures

Plaques—decorative pieces for walls. Wedgwood made luster plaques

*Plates—another big area for the beginner to explore. A collection can run through all the various chinawares, from early Historic Blue, etc., to the later commemorative plates of cities, events, and personages up to the calendar plates of the 1900's, a year to each plate, and the Gibson Girl subjects of the turn of the century. A collector might find it interesting to narrow down to portrait plates

Platters

Pomade jars—for creams, hair dressings, etc.

Potpourri jars—with perforated tops through which the spicy scent of dried flower leaves could escape

Powder boxes

Punch bowls

Ring trees—popular Victorian bureau piece, a china tree on the branches of which rings could be hung when not worn

Rose bowls—round vases with narrow opening for roses

*Shaving mugs—very popular collectible. Those personalized with owner's name and a picture of his occupation very expensive. Subjects run into the hundreds; 1860 to early

1900's. There are many others in china and pottery, and in various shapes, notably the scuttle shape. Some have shelf or compartment for soap

Souvenir pieces—marked with the name of a popular resort

Spittoons—mostly pottery and stoneware

*Steins—so-called because many were of German stoneware. Of these the Mettlach are the finest. But there were Dresden steins, Jasper, and other stoneware. A stein was a drinking mug of fairly large proportions. Another name was *becher*. An ornamental stein without handles made for communal, ceremonious purposes was called a *humpen*

*Stoneware

Jugs

Crocks

Bean pots

Batter jugs—with wire bail and spout for pancake batter

Butter crocks—when butter was kept in the springhouse or cellar

Milk basins—wide, shallow basins for skimming cream from milk

Water coolers—with faucets

Bellarmine jugs—a stone jar with a raised decoration of a bearded mask supposed to be the face of Cardinal Bellarmino. German

Vinegar jugs

Cider jugs

Churns

Foot warmers—hollow stoneware in various shapes for holding hot water. Used in sleighs and carriages

Washbasins and pitchers

Pitchers

Sugar bowls

Sugar shakers—with lids of pewter or silver

Syrup jugs

Tea caddies

*Teapots

Tea sets

*Tiles—used for hot dishes or plant stands, for around fire-
places, or for pure decoration. *Delft* tiles originated in
Holland. Were of Dutch faience ware with pictures in
blue or manganese purple. Subjects were biblical, ships,
landscapes, ladies, soldiers, playing children, etc. In
England delft tiles were made at Lambeth, Bristol, and
Liverpool. Later ones were transfer-printed. Most famous
is the Liverpool series of *Aesop's Fables*. Later tiles from
most of the Staffordshire potteries are not so expensive

Toast racks—a serving piece with a series of vertical compartments for holding toast

*Tobies—named for Toby Philipot, a jovial drinker in
Tristram Shandy. A jug caricaturing well-known characters, made by many English potters from 1743 on.
There were American Rockingham Tobies, too, from
Bennington, Greatbach, and many others. Lenox and
Onandaga made porcelain ones. Tobies were also made
in delft, silver luster, and Royal Doulton, which still
sends them over in all the old characters as well as
commemorative pieces such as Churchill, MacArthur,
etc.

*Trinket boxes—of these the most important collectibles are
the Staffordshire boxes made in many forms, bureaus,
washstands, melodeons, etc., or with figures of lambs,
Little Red Riding Hood, dogs, etc., on the lids. There
are, however, many other china boxes, Dresden, etc.,
many of which are less expensive for the beginner to
start with

Tureens

Vases and urns

Washstand sets—consisting of pitcher, bowl, small pitcher for
hot water, soapdish, toothbrush holder, shaving dish,
slop bucket, and chamber pot. Some of these are quite
handsome and can be found in many of the best china
wares. Individual pieces are easier to find than whole
sets

5. Advertising Items

These are items bearing the name of the manufacturer or made expressly for giveaways for publicity purposes. This collectible group pulls from many categories, such as:

Fans—giveaways distributed at funerals, put in church pews, and so on. Of folded paper or cardboard stuck in a crude wooden handle. Often amusing

*Transfer-printed tin—boxes, trays, and plates, right up to advertising items like the Coca-Cola trays, plates, etc.

Bootjacks—some of the iron ones were cast with an advertiser's name on them

Spool cabinets—for storing and displaying spool cotton in the stores. Each manufacturer got out his own. Many drawers

Paper dolls—giveaways to attract the children. Printed on the back, obtainable with soap wrappers, coffee coupons, etc.

Spoons

Thermometers

Calendars

*Advertising cards—from the late nineteenth century; a very popular collectible of the moment

All kinds of containers, with trade names on them

6. Animals

Not only animal figures but objects in animal shapes or showing pictures of the chosen animal.

Cats—chalkware. Staffordshire, other ceramics

*Dogs—all varieties. Famous are the Staffordshire spaniels in pairs, often with glass eyes, often spotted in luster. Also Staffordshire poodles with baskets in their mouths and greyhounds. Bennington made hounds and poodles, too. There were chalkware dogs.

Horses

Pigs

*Cows—add here the cow creamers, cream pitchers in the shape of cows made by many potters, notably Whieldon and in American Rockingham ware

Roosters and hens—in ceramics, carved wood, metal, and chalk-
ware
Mice
Rabbits
Lions
Elephants
Owls
*Birds
    Prints (see No. 51)
    Game plates
    Singing birds—usually caged with music boxes, or wind-ups
    Sewing birds—(see No. 48)
    Whistles—small china, pottery, or metal birds
*Eagles—a popular collectible. Most valued are those by Schim-
mel, an itinerant German woodcarver in Pennsylvania 1860–
90, by Bellamy in Maine around 1850, by names such as
Grier, Rush, and Skillin. In the 1880's Bakewell and Mullin
of Ohio manufactured metal eagles. There are also many
eagle motifs on china, glass, brass, etc.
Fish
Dolphins—a motif used frequently for standards for candlesticks,
compotes, etc.

7. Automobile Items

Aside from old cars there are many automobile accessories that
appeal to collectors.

Horns
Lamps
Handbooks and guides
Flower vases
Radiator caps
*License plates—early ones up to 1921 most valuable

8. Banks

Here is one of the top ten, particularly the mechanical banks.

Mechanical banks—there are approximately two hundred and fifty
known subjects in this category of iron banks (a few of tin)

made between 1870–1910, chiefly for children. They were
amusing and ingeniously fashioned to perform some trick
when a penny was deposited. Prices are astronomical, going
into the thousands for certain rare ones such as the *Harle-
quin, Clown and Columbine* bank. *Always Did 'Spise Dat
Mule* bank, fairly common, sells for around $40.00
*Still banks (iron)—penny banks that did not move, figures of
animals, buildings, people, etc. Rising in price but still
comparatively reasonable
*Still banks in other materials, pottery, glass, china, etc.
Book banks in Rockingham and other pottery
Cash register banks
Banks made for other purposes as well as for saving money

9. Bells

*Bells are very popular. Many collectors do not limit them-
selves to old bells or to American bells. Here are some of the
antique bells that collectors look for:

Sleigh bell—from the large brass Russian bells down to leather
straps with as many as forty bells riveted on. Better strings
have bells attached with shanks and cotter pins. Better bells
are engraved. A string of graduated bells very desirable
Harness bell—a series of larger bells on strap, usually in series of
five
Conestoga bell—used on the horses that drew the Conestoga
wagons. Of brass mounted on wrought-iron frame to be attached to the collar or hame. In sets of six, the two for the
lead horses having five bells, those for the next pair four
bells, and the bells for the two rear horses just three. Very
desirable. Getting rare
Store bell—the bell on a spring that tinkled when the door was
opened
School handbells—some very fine with curly-maple handles
Doorbell—a small gong set in the door to be operated from the
outside
Table bell—silver, brass, glass, china, a small handbell

Desk bell—a gong on stand with a push-down button
Ship bell
Fire-engine bell
Farm bell to mount on stand or in a small steeple
Slave bell—small bell on decorative stand struck with a wired hammer for summoning servants. Often of shell and metal
Church bells—altar bells, handbell type or in sets to be shaken during solemn parts of the Mass
Cow bell—rectangular metal to be hung around animal's neck. Swiss type
Sheep bell—smaller type of cow bell
Cat bell—small bell to tie on a ribbon on cat's neck
Bell toys—pull toys that rang a bell as they were moved
Rattles—with series of small bells on leather or a stick

10. *Birdcages*

A wider category than you might imagine.

Wicker
Wood—both primitive and decorative, some painted with applied gesso work
Wire
Wire and pierced metal
Brass
Figure shapes in wire
Styles that resembled houses
Chinese pagoda
Wheel—like small Ferris wheel in round frame
Period styles, Chippendale, Sheraton, etc.

11. *Bootjacks*

*Made to help gentlemen remove tight boots by catching the heel in the jack while the other foot held the jack firm.

Wooden—primitive shapes
Brass
Iron

Figural—Beetles, Pistol, Naughty Lady or Naughty Nellie (cor-
seted, tight-waisted shape)

12. *Boxes*

A fascinating collectible with plenty of opportunities for the
beginner who does not want to narrow down. Boxes to look for
are:

*Snuffbox—once as important as today's cigarette case. Snuffboxes
can be found in pewter, brass, bone, silver, horn, wood, with
engraving, transfer-printed pictures, painted. American historical snuffboxes with transfer-printed subjects on papier-
mâché very good

Patch box—to hold the small black cutout patches of "court
plaster" used as beauty spots on the face. Some of the finest
varieties of china, glass, enamel, and metal are found here

*Teabox—not only canisters made for storing tea but the inter-
esting small boxes that tea was sold in, many of Russian
origin

Candlebox—often of wood with sliding lid, or of tin to be hung
not too close to the fireplace

*Soapbox—for travelers. Of metal, often silver

Jewel box—hinged-lid box for bureaus

Collar box—for stiff collars, when shirts were made without collars

Cuffs box—for stiff cuffs, when cuffs were made separately

Stud box—for masculine use

Spool boxes—not the cabinets but small ones for the home sewer

Bandboxes—originally used for holding women's neckbands, caps,
fichus, etc. Put into use when traveling. Of light wood, round
or oval, painted or paper-covered. Brides' boxes were presents from the groom. The Pennsylvania Dutch excelled in
making these

*Hatboxes—round, paper-covered pasteboard boxes. Old ones
show samples of old wallpaper. Famous maker was a woman,
Hannah Davis. Often lined with old newspapers

Pillbox

*Cosmetic and drug boxes—interesting ceramic boxes with trans-
fer-painted pictures (particularly fine are the shaving soapboxes) or labels of the shops
Cigar box
Tobacco box—early Dutch and German boxes of etched brass
very good
Matchbox—(see No. 42)
*Spice box—usually in sets, often of japanned tin in a large tin
box container. Also the round or oval wooden boxes

13. *Brass*

*Cooking utensils
    Teakettles—rarer than copper. Early ones had pineapple
    knobs, serpent's head spout. Teakettles over spirit lamps
    for Victorian tea table are desirable
    Chafing dishes—many quite early
    Chocolate pots—often with straight wooden side handle
    Braziers—with wooden handles and iron legs—old
    Skillets—frying pans for open fire
    Skimmers—marked pieces rare
    Ladles—marked pieces rare
    Dippers—marked pieces rare
    Forks
    Drainers or colanders
Measures—graduated
Trivets (see No. 65)
Door knockers or door rappers—many fine Georgian styles
Buckets and pails—for water and milk
Candlesticks—period styles (require study). Later ones of cast
brass
Mortars and pestles—used by apothecaries for grinding drugs and
herbs. Also used in kitchen. Early ones brought over by
colonists from home country
Fireplace pieces
    Andirons—period styles (require study)
    Fenders—all brass or combined with wire
    Kettle stands

Footman—an English footed stand for the fireplace for keeping dishes warm

Tongs, shovels, and brushes with stands (often only handles were brass)

Jamb hooks—single or double hooks used at the side of a fireplace for hanging up the fire tools. Old ones very desirable

Coal boxes with lids

Coal hods—handled buckets

Warming pans—long-handled, round-lidded pans with decorative etched lid, often perforated, to hold hot coals for warming the bed sheets. Iron or wooden handles

Bellows—more often of wood, but also of brass. Used to pump air on a low fire or embers to bring it to a blaze

*Scales and weights—many kinds, apothecary, gold assayer's, etc.

Locks and keys—large rectangular door lock is called a carpenter or box lock

Furniture brasses—in all period styles (require study)

Samovars—large urn in brass or nickel over brass for hot water on tea table. Has faucet. Charcoal compartment heats the water. A Russian name often applied to tea urns

Tiebacks—to loop back long draperies from windows. Two types, the large rosette and the strap

*Door stops

Picture frames

Jardinières

Umbrella stands

Cuspidors

Urns

Plaques—decorative plates for wall

Wood boxes

Sundials

Weather vanes

Bells

Bible clasps and corners—for the large, family-type book

Horns

    Auto

Fireman's
Canalboat
Tallyho

14. *Bronzes*

Figures
Clock ornaments—used with marble clocks of the Victorian era,
  also on French clocks
Plaques
Wall ornaments

15. *Business Items*

Yes, these are collected by individuals as well as commercial
concerns.

Typewriters
Cash registers
Papyrographs—letter copiers
Letter scales
Check writers
Old ledgers
Letter presses
Mimeographs
Adders
Early fountain pens

16. *Buttons*

*One of the largest fields for collectors and the easiest to get
into. Buttons have been well classified, and the groups offer so
many varieties that it should not be hard to hit on many that
will not be too hard to find or cost much money. Here are only
a few of the buttons collectors talk about. To learn more read one
of the many good button books.

China
Glass
Metal
Painted
Wood

Enameled
Jeweled
Inlaid
Ivory
Fabric
Embroidered
Military
Dress
Costume
Ornament
Picture
Storybook
Historical
Circus
Yuletide
Silhouette
Shell
Zodiac
Animals
Insects
Marine
Drama
Calicoes—china buttons with calico patterns
Passementerie—trimmed braid or fabric button
Paperweight—with a figure embedded in plastic
Goofies—small novelty figure buttons, hats, animals, vegetables,
     etc.

Get a bird's-eye view of the field before you start and talk to
collectors and dealers before you pick your specialty. Join a button group and watch the magazines for button articles.

An interesting side line for buttoneers is *studs. In the shirt-
waist era many ornamental studs were made for women as well
as men, not all of gold or silver.

Included here, too, might be *buckles and clasps so often found
in the same boxes with old buttons. They can be a side line or a
full collectible on their own.

17. Christmas Items

*Christmas-tree ornaments and balls—old ones, many early balls
   were of blown glass
*Christmas-tree lights—see No. 3
Christmas angels
*Crèche figures—from old Nativity scenes, ceramic or carved wood
Putz figures—the putz was the Pennsylvania Dutch Christmas
   village. Often whittled from wood.
Santa Clauses
   Iron toy with sleigh and reindeer
   Bottle
   Molds
   Light bulbs
   Banks
   Cards
Danish Christmas plates (see No. 4)
Holly china
Souvenir spoons
*Madonnas—ceramic, wood, metal. Painted primitives
Music boxes—playing Christmas carols. Often part of a toy
Christmas cards

18. Clocks and Watches

*Clocks
   The collector who tackles the subject of clocks will not be
likely to narrow down to one kind because of the expense, scarcity, and storage room needed for old clocks, especially items such
as the early tall-case clocks. He might possibly graduate by degrees into specializing in one kind, such as shelf clocks, wall
clocks, dated clocks, novelty clocks, or perhaps clocks of certain
makers. But as a beginner he would be wiser to start his collection on a larger scale of choice with any clocks that struck his fancy
and read up before he began to specialize. Late clocks are, of
course, more plentiful and cheaper for the beginner, and there
are still many interesting pieces to be found among them.
   Here is a list that is not comprehensive, merely some sugges-

tions with definitions to show the range in the big world of time-keepers.

Tall-case clock—Grandfather clock. Case and works often made by two different people. Signed ones most desirable. Early ones had brass dials. Best years were the 1700's. Many books have been written on the famous clockmakers both English and American

Miniature tall-case, half tall-case, or grandmother clock—A short version of the tall clock, and sometimes used on shelves. Made shorter, so it is said, so a woman could reach it

Bracket clock—small clock for a shelf often made expressly for it

Lantern clock—English bracket or wall clock of brass shaped like a lantern. Also called birdcage clock

Wall clocks—many early varieties hung on the wall, using the long pendulum and without the tall case

Wag-on-the-wall clock—dial and works without a case with the pendulum swinging in view

Banjo clock—shaped like a banjo and made by early American clockmakers, particularly Willard

Steeple clock—double steeple—mantel clock with steeple finials at each side and gothic pointed case

O-G or O-O-G—named from the type of molding from which the rectangular case was made

Shelf clock—usually used to mean any type of American mantel clock

Pillar and scroll—type of case. Mantel clock

Railroad clock—large plain wall clock used in railroad stations

Lighthouse clock—clock enclosed in glass case at the top of a wooden base shaped like a lighthouse

Cuckoo clock—German or Swiss

Victorian mantel clock—of marble or ormolu, often bronze-trimmed. Resembling French clocks

China clock—particularly Dresden

Milk glass clock—small table or mantel clock

Wagon wheel—type of works

Wooden works—early clocks with wood instead of brass for works, made by such makers as Jonathan Frost, Chauncey Ives, Jerome and Darrow, etc.

Clocks in various shapes such as locomotives, ships, etc.

Clockmakers to be studied

Willard
Terry
Thomas
Jerome
Ansonia
Bristol
Waterbury

Watches

Here it is better to leave the older watches of English or Continental origin to the advanced collector and stick to the later watches, many of which can be found today. Date plays a great part in collecting watches. Below is a list of suggestions:

Keyless watches—1700
Second hand—1780
Double-case—having a protective case within outer decorative one
Open-face—1890
Railroad
Key winders
Chatelaine
Lady's pin-on watch
Grandpa's "turnip"
Early dollar watches
Early radium dial—1896
Early wrist watches—1917
Presentation watches
Watches that once belonged to well-known people
Trick watches—set into other articles

Related articles in the watch field

Watch chains
Watch keys

Watch fobs

Stop watches

*Watch stands—many ingenious ornaments for holding watch
when not in use. Metal, wood, ceramic

*Watch papers—discs slipped in the back case of a watch to
keep case and works from rattling and loosening

Advertising paper

Silk

Hand painted

Embroidered

Valentine

Time-telling Items

Hourglasses

*Calendars

Sundials

Pocket

Outdoor

19. *Copper*

Many pieces are combined with brass (see No. 13) and most of
the objects made in brass were made in copper, too. Add

Molds

Funnels

Powder flasks

Vases

Apple butter kettles—very large, used with paddles over outdoor fire

20. *Coronation and Commemorative Pieces*

Anything in silver, brass, glass, china, pottery, etc., brought
out to celebrate some special event. English pieces commemorat-
ing the coronation of English monarchs or other historical events
found their way to America among early imported English wares.
They are collectibles, but scarcely common enough to interest

the beginner. There are many others, however, to tempt the beginning collector.

Presidential items—from Washington on in glass, prints, buttons, china, textiles, etc.

Marriage certificates—these were part of the Pennsylvania Dutch art called *fractur*, elaborate hand-lettered and illuminated pieces recalling medieval manuscripts but much more primitive and crude. Later certificates were printed and then hand colored.

Many other old marriage certificates showed hand-painted decoration.

Birth records—

Fractur pieces—called *Geburtschein* or *Taufschein* (baptismal certificates)

Birth plates

Bible records

Spoons

Christening mugs, basins, etc.

Family trees

Commemorative plates of city and town or college anniversaries

Souvenirs of fairs and exhibitions such as the Centennial, World's Fair, etc.

Toby jugs of people in the news

21. *Costumes, Accessories, and Textiles*

Shawls

Cashmere—imported from India about 1777. Woven in the Vale of Kashmir from the wool of special goats. Beautiful woven and embroidered designs using exotic symbols of the East. As large as $3\frac{1}{2}$ by $1\frac{1}{2}$ yards

Paisley—made by Scotch weavers to imitate the expensive cashmere shawls, using Persian patterns

Lace

Chinese embroidered—1870's

Beaded

Plain woolen or plaid woolen—often worn by men

Mantilla—lace head veil and shawl

*Fans
> Chicken skin—a vellum or paper-thin parchment made from kid or lamb or swan skin. Painted like paper
> Painted paper
> Silk
> Lace
> Ivory—small folding fan with carved or openwork blades called a *brise* or *minuet* fan
> Feather—peacock, ostrich, turkey
> Sandalwood
> Fans with tortoise mountings
> Fans with mother-of-pearl mountings
> French fans—some of the finest done by Watteau, Boucher, etc.
> Spanish—often spangled
> Mourning—nineteenth-century American, black with jet or dark tortoise
> Novelty—Rosette fan that folds into the handle, originating with Japanese
> > Mask fan
> > Mirror fan

Laces and lace pieces
> Caps
> Fichus
> Christening robes
> Wedding veils
> Bobbin or pillow laces
> Crochet—filet or Irish
> Tatting
> Rare laces for advanced collectors

Parasols and umbrellas—interest lies in the handles though fabric should be preserved if possible

*Canes—a natural collectible for men

Band boxes

Hatboxes

Trunks

Portmanteaus or traveling cases

Carpetbags

Reticules

Miser's purses—a long purse with opening in the middle and rings
to keep contents secure in each end. When large could be
worn over the arm

*Calling-card cases—ivory, papier-mâché, tortoise, wood, silver

Combs and hair ornaments—of gold and silver, tortoise, and
pressed and carved cattle horn

Snoods—netted caps to restrain long hair-do

Mitts and gloves

Corsets

Buskboards—a stiff wooden or whalebone (scrimshaw) board worn
by women to give a "straight-front" figure

Bonnetieres—bonnet stands, often amusing papier-mâché heads
on stands with painted faces and named with a girl's name.
Used at home or in millinery shops

*Handkerchiefs—early ones of printed cotton. Historical hand-
kerchiefs go back as far as 1775. They were often campaign
items

Women's toilet accessories

    Shoebutton hooks and glove hooks

    Corset-lacers—hooks for tightening or loosening laces

    Curling irons—some made for traveling with spirit lamp

    Lorgnettes

    Corsage holders and corsage pins

    Train holders

    Veil clips

Men's accessories

    Monocles

    Key rings

    Dog whistles

    Shoehorns

    Mustache curlers

    Cravats

    Flasks

Bosom bottles—small perfume bottles to tuck into dress front

Muff bottles—small perfume bottles to carry in muff

Smelling salts bottles

Paper dress patterns

Textiles

Homespun

Handwoven linen

Old calicoes

Chintzes—copperplate chintzes printed in England in the 1700's and 1800's are very desirable as collectibles

Toile de Jouy—a linen or cotton printed fabric with a pictorial design in one color on a light ground

Tablecloths and napkins

Fringed towels

Marseilles spreads—popular in early 1900's. A heavy woven cotton cover in white, often quite elaborate in design

Any old dress or upholstery material

Remnants of old woven coverlets, rag carpets, etc.

22. Desk Accessories

*Inkwells—a wide area for collecting, silver, pewter, brass, iron, glass, china, papier-mâché, wood, many amusing novelties including old inkwells from school desks

Seals and sealing wax

Taper jacks—holders, often brass, for a thin coiled wax candle used for heating sealing wax

Stamp boxes—will not date any earlier than the last half of the 1800's

Sanders—pewter, silver, iron, tin, brass, china, wood, used to sprinkle sand for absorbing the ink before blotters were made

Paper knives—wide variety here

Spring paper clips—many interesting ones in Victorian brass, including the familiar hand motif

Scales

Memo books

Pens—early nibs, also lady's pens of gold and pearl-handled

Retractible pencils—go back as far as early 1800's. Some have jewels set in ends

Pen trays

Paperweights
    Glass (see No. 3)
    Metal—iron, brass, German silver
    Novelty
Slates—single and double
School companions—pencil boxes, often quite decorative in wood
    or composition

23. *Dolls and Doll Items*

*This is one of the largest areas of collecting and, like buttons,
it should be gone into with some study before you begin. If you
intend to go after the old ones, here is a classification usually
recognized by the big doll shows:

1. Wooden
        Queen Anne
        Georgian Period
        Other seventeenth- and eighteenth-century dolls
        Dutch dolls
        Penny woodens
        Pegged woodens
        Primitives
        Homemades
        Hand carved
        Joel Ellis and other Springfield dolls—Ellis was the
            first to make an articulated wooden doll with
            mortise and tenon joints, 1873
        Schoenhuts—from the Philadelphia toy firm, 1911–24
2. Wax
        Early wax dolls up to 1825
        Wire-eyed wax dolls
        Montanari—English, 1851
        Pierotti—English, 1790–1935
        Wax-coated—over composition
3. Papier-mâché
        Late 1700's up to 1825

Milliners' models—foreign imports to bring to the
   United States the latest fashions in clothes and
   hairdressing, 1820–60
French papier-mâchés
Superiors, Weigands, and others—1825–75
Pre-Greiner
Greiner—well-known German dollmaker who took
   out a patent for a papier-mâché doll in Phila-
   delphia in 1855
   Early unlabeled
   Labeled and unlabeled 1885–72
Character
Glass-eyed
4. Composition
   Nineteenth-century Schilling and contemporary
   Character dolls up to 1890—representing real people,
      particularly children
5. China
   Early
      Wooden bodies
      Cloth bodies
      Glass eyes with molded painted hair
   With wigs
      Biedermeier—German 1815–50
      Fancy hair-dos
   French chinas with cork pates and wigs
   Rare chinas
      Sleeping-eyed
      Swivel-necked
6. Parian bisque or Dresden-type bisque
   Plain undecorated—molded hair
   Decorated with hair and chest decorations
7. True Parian
   Early undecorated
   Decorated, fine quality
8. German bisque
   Lady or gentleman dolls up to 1890

Child dolls up to 1890
After 1890

9. French bisque
   Lady or gentleman dolls
   French fashion dolls—made to show fashions of late
   1800's
   French child dolls
   Bru—name of maker of French bisque dolls
   Jumeau—name of maker of French bisque dolls
   1862–98
   Steiner—made in Germany, assembled in France

10. Mechanical dolls
    Motion, no music
    Music, no motion
    Music and motion

11. Bonnet dolls
    All dolls with hat or bonnet molded in one with the
    head

12. Religious dolls
    Crèche—wax, wood, or terra cotta
    Church or shrine

13. Pedlar—nineteenth century or earlier of carved wood
    carrying a tray or basket of miniature articles

14. Fortune-telling—nineteenth century or earlier

15. Rag or fabric
    Primitive or homemade
    Commercial—many were printed on cotton to be cut
    out, sewn, and stuffed

16. Rawhide and leather—nineteenth century and earlier

17. Rubber and gutta percha—nineteenth century and earlier

18. Portrait—representing famous people such as Queen Vic-
    toria, Jenny Lind, etc.

19. Baby
    Early swaddling type
    Nineteenth century
    Twentieth century

20. Frozen Charlotte—one-piece, not articulated. So called

after a girl in an old Vermont ballad who froze stiff in a sleigh because she would not cover her party dress with a robe

21. Negro
22. Flirting-eyed—eyes move from side to side
23. Pumpkin head—heads with molded pompadours and a circular band like a comb to give a pumpkin shape
24. Named doll
25. Chinese
26. Kewpies—from the Rose O'Neill character created in early 1900's
27. Kathe Kruse—a fabric doll made in Germany before and after World War II
28. Storybook dolls
29. Dolls for other uses, such as tea cozies, telephone covers, pincushions, string holders

*Paper dolls
    Homemade
    Commercial
    French
    McLaughlin—made by Massachusetts printing firm in mid-1800's
    Raphael Tuck—English
    Godey's Lady's Book cutouts
    Later cutouts
    English Queens series—rather rare
    Ballet
    Military
    Theatrical
Paper doll furniture
Pantins—paper dolls articulated and made to move with wires, string, or heat from a stove, or candle, jumping jacks, etc.
Puppets
    Hand
    String
Doll clothes
Doll clothes patterns

Doll accessories—earrings, fans, purses, gloves, parasols, etc.
Doll furniture
Doll dishes
Doll carriages
Dollhouses
Dollhouse furniture
Toy pianos—particularly Schoenhut
Toy theaters
Toy stores

24. Eggs

This is an amusing idea to follow up.

Darning eggs
Nest eggs
Blown and dyed Easter eggs
Easter eggs with inside panorama
Egg cups
Chicken and egg dishes
Egg cookers
Egg servers—table pieces in silver or china with cups or holders
    for eggs and spoons
Sewing kits in eggs
Perfume containers in eggs
Russian Easter eggs—Fabergé—very costly. Enameled and jeweled

25. Enamels

Fabergé—made by Russian goldsmith of late 1800's—exquisite—
    costly
Battersea—Eighteenth-century enamels painted on copper base.
    Usually bright colors on yellow. Also transfer-printed. Not
    for the beginner
Staffordshire—made by Staffordshire artists after closing down of
    Battersea. Slightly more available
French enamels
European cloisonné—1870–1900
Articles found in enamel
    Patch boxes

Snuffboxes
Mirror knobs
Spoons
Wine labels
Perfume bottles
Etuis—small cases for sewing or toilet accessories
Boxes shaped like birds, human heads, animals
Trinket boxes
Buttons
Crosses
Watch cases
Toothpick cases
Eggs

26. *Figures and Figurines*

*Staffordshire chimney pieces—made for the popular market
Staffordshire cottages—ceramic houses, castles, etc., for ornaments,
    banks, watch holders, or in which pastilles could be burnt
Toby jugs
Bennington flint-enamel figures
Bennington Parian—white unglazed, looks like marble
Other Parian—some good, later Victorian not so good. Many busts
Chalk—really plaster of Paris
    Pieces made over Staffordshire figure models
    Pieces attributed to the Pennsylvania Dutch
*Bisque—unglazed hard-paste china. Most available are Victorian
*Rogers Groups—created by John Rogers around 1860, realistic
    figure groups, eighty subjects, many pertaining to Civil War
    and everyday life. Painted in dull putty colors. Most popular
    were *The Checker Players, Coming to the Parson,* and Lin-
    coln's *Council of War*
Potty figures—amusing, slightly naughty, of little children
Bronze figures
Ivory
Orchestras—composed of monkey or dwarf figures, each playing a
    different instrument
Busts of famous people

*Nodders—figures with heads balanced on wire to keep nodding when set in motion. Some were toys

27. Firearms

*A highly specialized field that breaks down into many categories. Advanced gun collectors are dedicated. But it is an irresistible hobby for men and boys, and one has to begin somewhere. Again it is a good idea to read the books for guidance. There are many. Here is a brief view of the field:

Rifles and long guns—from early flintlocks and muskets through the Kentucky or Pennsylvania rifle made in Lancaster, Pennsylvania, before the Revolution through the Civil War period and the big names of the 1880's such as Sharp, Springfield, Winchester, Remington, Stevens, Marlin, etc.

Pistols and revolvers—from the blunderbuss through the Colts and Remingtons and Derringers and including such special items as dueling pistols, gamblers' pistols, muff pistols, stagecoach pistols, target pistols, etc.

Cartridges

Bullet molds

*Powder flasks and shot bottles

Cannons—real ones and the models made for them

28. Fire-fighting Items

*Fire marks—the marks of the early insurance companies made to put on the front of a dwelling to indicate that it was insured and guide the fire brigades, often to insure preference from them. Most of the marks were iron but some were of lead on wood or even of terra cotta. The Green Tree of Philadelphia and the Hand-in-Hand early and desirable

Buckets—leather buckets, deep and bailed for carrying the water. Often elaborately decorated and showing the name of the owner or of the fire company

Helmets

Firemen's buttons

Horns and trumpets

Bells—from old engines
Lamps—from old engines
Hatchets
Shields—from the uniforms or hats
Music
Painted panels from old engines

29. *Flowerpots and Vases*

Crocus pots—for bulbs
Cache pots—to hold flowerpots, usually in porcelain or tole
Bough pots—old name for vase for cut flowers or branches
Jardinières—many fine china and stoneware items, even Wedgwood
Flowerpots—terra cotta or redware, sometimes decorated
Strawberry jars—with shelved openings on the sides in which single plants could be planted
Five-finger vases—a divided vase with five finger-like openings on a single standard like a spread-out hand
Hyacinth jars—of colored glass, deep enough for growing a single bulb in pebbles and water
Ferneries—brass, silver, etc., with inset of china or metal for table centerpieces
Iron plant stands—for a series of flowerpots. Often of wirework
Iron plant bracket—a swinging arm for a flowerpot

30. *Games*

*Playing cards—beginner can progress through fairly modern novelty cards back to the earliest examples of the playing card in the sixteenth century
Card tables—in period styles up to the Victorian. Old game tables had pockets for chips or money called "scoops" and dished candle disks at each corner called "reserves." Tops often covered with leather or felt
Chips—very fine ones were of mother-of-pearl
Game boards—for backgammon, chess, etc.
Chess pieces—a favorite collectible, running from Chinese carved ivory to primitive homemade items. Often made by prisoners

Dominoes—some old sets were carved from bone. Many home-
    made
Dice
Jack straws
Mah-jongg—the Chinese game popular in early 1900's. Still played
Jigsaw puzzles—there were old ones, too
Bible games—many quite early, played with cards
*All the old games of 1890–1910
    Tiddlywinks
    Fish Pond
    Old Maid
    Snap
    Pin-ons—the "donkey-tail" game

31. *Horse Items*

*Brasses—decorative brass disks hung on the harness as amulets to
    ward off the evil eye. Also to denote ownership. Early ones
    very fine. Many reproductions
*Bridle rosettes or buttons—decorative buttons of metal, glass,
    etc., to dress up the bridle. Great variety
Hames bells (see No. 9)
Branding irons
Currycombs—many old ones show ornamental carving
Spurs
Whips
Stirrups
Saddles
Prints of famous horses
Ribbons and trophies
Jockey caps
Hitching posts

32. *Iron*

Hardware—for house and cabinet. Early wrought-iron hinges,
    latches, locks, bolts, hooks, shutter guards, chest handles,
    chest hinges, Conestoga hinges, etc. Any old iron is a good

buy, but for anyone who intends to specialize in it study is
advised

Weather vanes—iron vanes were often quite primitive. They
showed such designs as dates, initials, Indians, cocks, arrows,
ships, fish, plows, and tulips

Door knockers—many of the iron ones were as handsome as the
brass ones. A novelty was the knocker latch, a combination
of knocker which could be turned to lift inside latch

Shelf brackets

Scrolls and supports for signs and lamps

Andirons—early and primitive, include the famous Hessian figures and other figures, serpentine and heart finials

    Creepers—small irons placed between the larger ones for
small logs

    Spit—andirons with hooks across which spits could be laid

*Fireplace accessories

    Cranes—swinging arms to hold cooking vessels over fire

    Trammels—notched bars for cranes to lower and raise pots
over fire

    S-hooks—on which to fasten the bail of the pot on trammel
or directly on crane

    Spits—an apparatus on which meat was roasted by a turning
rod, operated by hand, dog, or clockwork

    Toasters—flat and upright

    Waffle irons—some in heart shape

    Wafer irons—making wafers for church service

    Spiders—frying pan with legs

    Cat—six-legged stand that could be set on either end

    Trivets (see No. 65)

    Tongs

    Shovels and peels—a peel was a flat shovel for removing
baked goods from oven

    Broilers

    Pipe tongs—for holding hot ember to light pipe

    Skewer sets and holders—show fine craftsmanship

Lighting (see No. 37)

Bells (see No. 9)

Gophering irons—for ironing and pleating ruffles—two varieties, one like a poker, the other corrugated to roll over a similarly corrugated stand

Pressing irons—old ones heated by coals in the bottom—others on top of stove. Miniature ones desirable

*Cooking utensils—forks, ladles, pots, pans, muffin pans, etc.

Fire marks (see No. 28)

Snow birds—small birds, like eagles, used along the roof to hold back an avalanche of heavy snow

Hitching posts and heads

Humidifiers or stove vases—topped the parlor stove and were kept full of water. Often found alone. Reproduced

Stove plates—sides of early six-plate and ten-plate stoves of box shape. Often quite elaborately designed

Firebacks—plates used at the back of a fireplace to protect wall and deflect heat. Early ones executed by German artists. Very fine

Door stops—many in animal shapes

Scales—old store scales, large ones for weighing out bags of feed and meal, counter scales with tin or brass scoops

Gypsy pots—round three-legged pot for open-fire cooking

Foot scrapers—various styles for imbedding in wall or doorstep for cleaning muddy shoes

Coal baskets—for open-grate coal fires

Coal scuttles—for carrying coal

Match safes

String holders—from old stores. To hold ball of string with hole for the end to be pulled through

Bill hooks—spikes for filing bills or papers, also used in old stores and offices

*33. *Jewelry*

Amber
Agate
Garnet
Jet
Onyx

Hair—all kinds of ornaments were woven from human hair as mementoes or memorials

Tortoise

Cameos—any stone with carved raised design in contrasting relief. Stone with colored layers is usually used

Intaglios—design is incised on stone or gem. Used for seals

Mosaic—design inlaid with colored stones on dark ground, often onyx

Bog oak—black, very hard wood, carved for jewelry. Irish or English

Beads—glass, metal, ceramic, wood, jet, amber

Scarf and stickpins—men's

Hatpins

Earring or opera cases—small hinged cases to slip around the jewels of valuable earrings

Chain slides—from long gold chains binding strands together

Chains

Chatelaines—clipped or pinned at belt to hold variety of small objects—pencils, keys, watches, charms, vinaigrettes, needle cases, etc.

Vinaigrettes—perforated boxes or bottles in which cotton soaked with aromatic vinegar was carried to revive fainting ladies

Bangles

Watch-chain accessories—seals, knives, watch keys, etc.

Watch fobs

Seals

Studs

Cuff links

Lockets

Earrings

Brooches

Bracelets

Necklaces

34. *Kitchen Items*

*Coffee mills—every kitchen had one long before the days of ready-ground coffee. A handle turned the grinder knives. A

small drawer caught the ground coffee. Those with pewter or brass cups where the coffee bean was poured in are considered best. Some were made small enough to be held on the lap, others were attached to the wall. There were grinders of iron, quite primitive, and in all woods, mostly pine and maple. In the stores these were turned by a side wheel, sometimes with two side wheels

*Mortars and pestles—used for spices, herbs, loaf sugar, etc. Large ones were used for grinding grains. They were made of wood, maple, burl, lignum vitae, of iron, brass, bell metal, bronze, and marble

Spice cabinets—usually a series of tiered drawers, occasionally combined with a hinged-lidded bin for salt, sugar, or flour

Salt boxes—standing or wall boxes of wood or ceramic or both

Spoon racks—decorative primitive pieces with notched shelves for displaying spoons and other table pieces

*Baskets

Willow baskets—woven from specially grown willow

Splint baskets—thin layers split from wood

Straw baskets—made from straw or grass bound into ropes

Sweet grass baskets—sweet-smelling grass in ropes

Egg baskets—with two-part rounded bottom

Bottle baskets

Clothesbaskets

Market baskets

Cradles—basinettes—like large clothesbasket with hooded end

Basket measures

Work baskets

Easter baskets

Woodenware—bowls, spoons, plates, measures

Small wire items—fruit baskets, potato baskets, egg baskets

Rolling pins—glass, wood, springerle (fancy molds for Christmas cookies)

Molds

Pottery

Pewter

Tin

*Copper
China jelly molds
Cheese molds—perforated ceramic or tin in which curds were
    pressed
*Wooden cookie or springerle molds
Marzipan—for making a candy or sweet cake of almond paste
    in various shapes
*Tin cooky cutters
Pie crimpers—for fancy edges on pies
Nutmeg graters
*Butter stamps and molds
Nutcrackers
Mousetraps
Fly traps
*Measures—pewter, tin, wood, copper
Old tools and gimmicks—apple parers, cherry-stoners, pea-shellers

*35. Knives

Bowie knives
Hunting knives
Dirks
Swords
Bayonets
Army knives
Pocket knives
Farm knives—sickles, corn knives, machetes
Skinners' knives
Tools for carving

36. Lacquer and Papier-Mâché

Lacquer is a colored and very hard varnish on wood. Objects
so treated were usually decorated—Chinese designs predominated.
Papier-mâché was made from paper pulp mixed with other things
to make a hard substance that could be sawed. Decorative, often
embellished with mother-of-pearl

Furniture
 Tea tables
 Tip-top tables
 Cabinets
 Fire screens
 Chairs
 Sewing stands
Lap desks
Writing portfolios
Albums
Bracket shelves
Snuffboxes
Jewel boxes
Patch boxes
Card cases
Card trays
Tea caddies
Drapery tiebacks
Buttons
Vases
Paper and book racks
Fans
Inkstands

37. *Lamps and Lighting Fixtures*

Rushlights—primitive iron stands with various kinds of clasps for holding a bunch of rushes dipped in grease

Fat lamps—an early lard or whale-oil lamp of britannia on acorn-, lemon-, urn-, cylinder-, or hexagonal-shaped bowl with or without saucer base

Betty lamps—early American oil lamp shaped like ancient vessels with a wick laid in the small end. Of iron or tin. Usually hung with a chain to an iron stand or hung from the ceiling

Peg lamp (see No. 3)

Whale-oil lamps—lamps used before the discovery of kerosene in 1859. Many of these were Argand lamps with tubular wick and a side reservoir for the oil

Angle lamps—with side arms for burner and reservoir

Kerosene lamp bases—these were made in all the popular glass, china, and metal styles of the late 1800's. You will find them in tin, pewter, brass, china, Sandwich glass, many of the pressed-glass patterns, and in colored and milk glass

*Miniature or night lamps—small versions of the larger kerosene lamps

*Fairy lamps—night lights with a thick candle in a saucer over which a glass shade is inverted

Astral lamp—a kind of Argand lamp made so that the flattened ring-shaped cistern for the whale oil did not interfere with the light on the table

Banquet lamp—a tall parlor lamp

Piano lamp—tall enough to shed light on the music. Sometimes it could be raised or lowered in the metal shaft of the stand

Hanging lamp

  Hall—early ones were lanterns, very elegant for candles. Later ones had small oil lamps

  Store—crude, usually brass in an iron frame with painted tin shade

  Library—for parlor or dining-room central lighting. Fairly elaborate in a Victorian way

  Pulley type—on chains which could be raised or lowered over the table

Student lamp—brass lamp with one or two arms. Oil reservoir separate from burner or burners and higher

Rochester lamp—lamp of the 1880's with a cylinder and collar and flat ring-type wick

Gone-with-the-wind lamp—facetious name for a fancy late Victorian parlor lamp with round glass shade and often a matching glass oil bowl

Carriage and hearse lamps

Bicycle lamp

Post lamps

Street lamps

Pullman lamps—bracketed ceiling lamps from old Pullman cars

Miners' lamps

Bracket lamps—lamps on swinging iron brackets. Sometimes with
    metal reflectors
Lampshades
    Ball
    Canopy
    Painted
    Art glass
    Lithophanes
    Cut glass
    Milk glass
Lanterns
    Candle
    Oil
    Stable
    Railroad
    English birdcage—of tin and wire with glass sides
    Ship—usually semicircular with flat back to hang against wall
    Dietz—name of famous manufacturer, still in business
    Pierced tin—so-called Paul Revere
    Brass
    Policeman's
    Post—of various types, often discarded old street lighting
*Candlesticks and candelabra
    Brass—these go back very far and can be found in all the
        periods in both socket and pricket (with spike for the
        candle) type. It needs study to recognize the character-
        istics. Later cast-brass sticks are available for the casual
        collector, although early ones of spun brass are the finest
    Silver
    Pewter
    Sheffield
    Tin
    China
    Pottery
    Taper sticks—a miniature stick for holding thin candles
    Chamber sticks—with saucer and handle for carrying up to
        bed

Unusual—many novelties. A collector might specialize in one
of a kind and find many surprises

Candle sconces—side lights for the wall of pewter, tin, brass, mirrored, with tin reflectors, even of ceramic as of Chinese Export china

Chandeliers—while one would not collect these exclusively, they
offer an interesting choice to include in a collection of lighting equipment, especially the old pieces

    Iron

    Tin

    Brass

    Crystal

    With burners of kerosene lamps

    Wood—carved and gilt, also in primitive forms

    For gaslight

Candle snuffers

Candle shields

Gas shades in fancy colored and etched glass including hobnailed,
cranberry, etc.

Smoke bells

Taper pots—holders for the supply of thin wax candles

Spill vases

Early electric bulbs

40. *Liquor Items*

Wine bottles

Stone gin or ginger-beer bottles

Liquor bottles

Decanters

Steins

Beakers—large drinking mugs

Measures

Flip glasses—early glass made when flip was a popular drink—like
a large flaring tumbler

Whisky tumblers

*Wineglasses—wide area here from early blown to cut glass

Beer glasses

Punch bowls and punch cups
Eggnog and toddy cups
Wine coolers—or wine cisterns like *Cellarettes,* for storing wine
bottles at table. Small wooden tubs, lead-lined, usually of
mahogany. Fine pieces of furniture
Liquor cases—for sets of liquor bottles, kept on sideboard or
library table, often camouflaged to look like a set of books
Monteiths—a bowl with notched or scalloped edge over which
wineglasses could be hung to cool in water. Named for a
Scotchman who supposedly wore a cloak with a scalloped
border
Wineglass coolers or basins—two-lipped bowls, like large finger
bowls, for cooling individual glasses at table
Bottle labels—paper ones hard to preserve, but they offer an in-
teresting field for collectors
Wine labels—for hanging on the decanters
Wine tasters—small silver bowl or spoon for tasting wine
Wine lists
Old tavern licenses
Old barroom signs and price lists
Temperance prints (Currier and Ives especially)
Old drink recipes
Mugs—odd drinking mugs for beer, rum, etc.
Cordial sets—decanter and small glasses usually on a matching
tray

41. *Masonic and Other Fraternal Items*

Chinese Export china
Engraved glass pieces
Flasks
Presentation pieces
Shaving mugs
Mustache cups
Cups and saucers
Paperweights

*42. *Match Holders*

Glass

China
Painted tin
Iron
    Standing
    Hanging
Novelty
Pocket match holders

43. *Military Items*

Guns (see No. 27)
Cannon—yes, these have been collected, including the small
    models made for large cannon
Hats and caps—hat emblems
Buttons—uniform
Insignia
Epaulettes
Medals and decorations
Belts and buckles
Holsters
Spurs
Bullet molds and bullet pouches
Shot cases
Powder horns
Flags
Batons
Drums
Cartridge boxes
Discharge papers
Canteens—flasks
Food containers
Camp candlesticks—came apart to pack compactly
*Toy soldiers
Military ceramic figures
Uniform prints
Battle scenes on china, prints, etc.
Maps

44. *Mirrors*

Courting mirrors—small mirrors about eighteen inches high with decorative glass border inside frame. Imported from China *c.* 1800.

Shaving mirrors—small mirrors on stands

Hand mirrors

Pocket mirrors

Mirrored objects, such as trinket boxes, fans, etc.

45. *Motifs*

An interesting slant for a collection that might include many things in glass, ceramics, metal, wood, etc.

*Hands—a very popular collectible that extends to many things, such as vases, compotes, calling-card trays, seals, door knockers, jewelry, prints, etc. While it was a common Victorian conceit, it goes back much further and the collector has a wide field to choose from

Feathers—incorporated in many designs, old and new

Shells

Tulips

Roses

Violets

Ferns

Other flowers

Fans

Hearts

Wedding rings

Beehives and bees

Pineapples

Snakes

Patriotic

    Flags

    Liberty Bell

    United States Seal

    Statue of Liberty

Eagle
Stars
Zodiac symbols

46. *Music*

Hand organs—roller organs
Street organs—roller organs
Chautauqua organs
Melodeons—small parlor organs, about 1850
*Music boxes
  Swiss
  American Regina
  Objects such as steins, albums, small jewel boxes, birds, etc.
  Coin boxes
Discs—used in boxes, a tune to each
Rolls—spiked rolls that made the tunes
Piano-player rolls
Old phonographs
*Phonograph records
Zithers
Harps
Violins
Mouth organs
Ocarinas—"sweet potatoes"
Jew's-harps
*Sheet music
Songbooks
Hymnals
Metronomes—pendulum instruments to tick the time for piano
  students
Music stands

47. *Nautical*

*Ship models
Ships in bottles
Ship prints
Compasses
Barometers

Other navigation instruments
Telescopes
Bells
Clocks
Lanterns
Navigation maps and charts
Ships' logs
*Clipper-ship cards
Figureheads—carved wooden figures from the prows of whaling
   ships
Whaling gear

48. *Needlework and Handwork*

*Samplers—early ones are narrow. Display of juvenile sewing skill
Coverlets—woven in colored wools on linen warp, 1830–50
Quilts—pieced, patched, appliqué. Study the old patterns
Quilt patches
Quilting patterns—cut from cardboard or tin
Hooked rugs—primitive
Hooked rug patterns—by Edward Frost, later by Pond from Bid-
   deford, Maine, and the Ross Rug Co. in 1885. Any amateur
   patterns
Embroidered pictures—in wool or silk on linen and satin. Some go
   back to 1700. They were "seminary" work in the early 1800's
Mottoes—worthy sayings like *God Bless Our Home* worked in wool
   on perforated cardboard and framed in rustic walnut
Tea cozies
Peasant embroideries
Netting for tester beds—for canopies and bed coverings
Show towels—elaborate, embroidered, lace-trimmed, and fringed
   towels for display beside the door or hung over the family
   roller towel when company came in Pennsylvania Dutch
   households
Articles made from old stitches such as needlepoint, flame stitch
   (sometimes called Bardello or Hungarian stitch), etc., including purses, men's slippers, spectacle cases, needlecases,
   chair seats, bell pulls, etc.

Berlin work—wool work done on printed patterns imported into this country from Germany 1835–70

Turkey work—wool knotted on canvas to imitate oriental carpets for eighteenth-century floor coverings

Braided rugs

Tatting

Crochet work

Embroidered centerpieces—eyelet, cutwork, solid work in white on linen or fruit and flower designs done with lustrous silks. Early 1900's

Bedspreads—crocheted or knitted

Embroidered pillow shams—day covers for bed pillows

Embroidered "splashers"—for back of washstands to protect wall

Wool-and-silk embroidered lambrequins—drapery for mantelpieces, often on felt

Bobbins and shuttles

Netting shuttles

Needles in packets—old

Pins—old

Needlecases—many novelties here, both homemade and otherwise

*Pincushions—a rewarding collectible including all homemade ones, embroidered, beaded, with silver chains and clips for wearing on a chatelaine, novelties of all kinds

*Thimbles

Scissors

Bodkins

Sewing birds—mounted on vise to screw on edge of table with beak of bird acting as a spring to grasp the cloth and hold it taut while it is being seamed. Some have pincushions, some are of pewter, others of white metal. Interesting collectible

Workbaskets and boxes

Spool cabinets and boxes

Beadwork—very popular handwork in the late 1800's. Used for purses, bell pulls, chair seats, etc.

Waxwork—early work was figure work and portraits done by artists, later wax was employed for molding the fruits and flowers kept under glass for the Victorian parlor

Featherwork—feathers were dyed and made into flowers for
    bouquets or for wreaths under glass
Shellwork—another late 1800 fad, used for decorating boxes,
    frames, and making flowers and wreaths out of small shells
Quillwork—goes back very early. Pictures and hatchments (coats
    of arms) were made by combining "quills" of tightly rolled
    colored papers with wax, tinsel, etc.
Scissors work—cutout pictures, often very detailed. Related to
    silhouettes. Called *Papyrotamia*
Tinsel pictures—pasted-up pictures from patches of colored tinsel
    papers
Decoupage—cutout motifs from printed pages or paper pasted on
    surface to make pictures or designs. Sometimes a whole piece
    of furniture was so treated. A French art, but practiced in
    America, too
Decalcomania—a gummed picture for transferring to any surface
    as decoration by soaking picture from backing
Hairwork—human hair braided into chains for watches and
    bracelets and woven into earrings, pins, etc., 1860–70

48. Optical Items

Eyeglasses
Lorgnettes
Monocles
Sunglasses
Opera glasses
Magnifiers
Binoculars
Telescopes or spyglasses
Periscopes
Kaleidoscopes—a toy. Tube with bits of colored glass in the bot-
    tom and lens which, when shaken, could show up many
    different geometric patterns
Zoetropes—for "moving pictures." A revolving drum with slots
    behind which a roll of pictures was passed (on same principle
    as movie film) to give the semblance of motion. Many varia-
    tions of this toy with other names

Magic lanters and slides
Stereopticons and cards
Cameras

50. *Popular Oriental Importations*

*Chinese Lowestoft—more properly called Chinese Export china. Very popular collectible, but while available quite expensive

Canton—imported to Europe in the 1700's. Scarcely for the beginner, unless he has some inherited pieces to start with

Rose Medallion—a favorite with collectors at the moment. A Chinese pattern with flowers and figures in panels. Sometimes called Rose Canton

Ivories—carvings

Netsuke—figures of ivory, wood, metal, or porcelain on a cord to serve as a button between the kimono and girdle to hold a money pouch. Japanese

Fans

Noritake China—(see No. 4)

Cloisonné—enamel on copper developed by Japanese in nineteenth century

Japanese Imari—the china that inspired so many European wares in the 1700's right down to the Pennsylvania Gaudy Dutch. It was a colorful porcelain in patterns copied from rich Japanese brocades. Worked its way to China and got to Europe and England with the big tea companies. Real Imari pieces are still available

Japanese lanterns—paper lanterns used with candles for outdoor festivals not too long ago

Terra cotta—ornaments

51. *Paintings, Prints, and Other Art Forms*

Primitive scenes and portraits—in oils, water colors, crayons, and chalks done on wood, tin, canvas, ticking, sacking, glass, or silk, by untrained artists. Crudity and sincerity appealing

*Silhouettes—cutout profile portraits in black on white or hollow-cut on black background by machine. Often filled out with water color or printed background. Flourished in late 1700's and early 1800's

Miniatures—portraits on ivory, china, lids of fine boxes, etc., by
the best professionals

*Paintings on glass—reversed paintings, done on the back of the
glass, a special kind of art used for clock-case inserts, mirror
frames, portraits, other picture subjects. Chinese were very
adept at this. Glass paintings were popular among the Pennsylvania Dutch, also in New England. It was one of the
"seminary" arts for young ladies of the early 1800's. Transfer
printing was also done on glass

Wood engravings

*Lithographs—a process of printing pictures from stone made
popular in this country from about 1830 on. First and greatest exponent was N. Currier, later Currier and Ives. Better
read up on this before starting to collect, as some subjects
run into the hundreds and thousands, others go for as low as
$5.00. Other names to look for are Prang, Kellogg, Duval,
Sarony, and Major, Haskell and Allen and many others,
1850–1900

Prints—a specialized field that needs study
  Bird—pre-Audubon, Audubon, Gould, Wilson, Pope, etc.
  *Flowers—from floral almanacs, catalogues such as Mrs.
      Wirt's, Dr. Thornton, Cassino, Dewey, Landreth. Fairly
      reasonable and worth investigating by the beginner
  Fruit—from old nursery catalogues
  Historical views
  *American scenes—New York, Philadelphia, Newport, Mis-
      sissippi, Western
  Cities
  Indians—many famous Indian chiefs let themselves be painted
  Street cries—Wheatley's *Cries of London* are famous and
      somewhat costly. But there were American street cries
      also
  *Fashion—*Godey's, Petersen's,* and *Leslie's,* French fashion
      magazines
*Fractur—
  Old hand-lettered and hand-painted pieces
  Later printed pieces

    Birth certificates
    House blessings
    Marriage certificates
    Merit cards
    Book plates
Shaker religious spirit drawings
Pinpricked pictures
Paintings on velvet
Theorems—stencils
Wax portraits
*Lithophanes
Signs
    Shop
    Inn
Fireboards—decorated panels to close up fireplace when not in
    use
Over-mantel pictures on panels
Scrimshaw
Banners—trade, political, Masonic (sometimes transparent)
Painted windowshades
Screens—paneled
Fire screens or pole screens could be raised or lowered to protect
    face against heat of fire or candle flame

52. *Paper Items*

Called *ephemera* by collectors.

*Maps
Geographies and atlases, particularly county atlases
Scrapbooks
Valentines (see No. 67)
*Christmas cards
*Post cards—very popular, many classifications
    Christmas
    Easter
    St. Patrick's Day
    July 4th

Thanksgiving
    Florals
    Greetings
    Comic
    Patriotic
    Parades
    Presidents
    Disasters
    Foreign
    Resorts and other localities
    Tinseled
Posters
    Theater
    Circus
    Carnival
    Rodeos
    Wild West shows
Programs
    Theater
    Recital
    Lecture
Handbills
Almanacs
*Newspapers—those announcing some big event are most valuable
Magazines
Diaries
Invitations
Letters
Menus
Bookplates
Documents
Deeds
Diplomas
Charts
Copybooks
Ledgers

Timetables
Trade cards
Labels
Calling cards
Lottery tickets
Bridge tickets
Toll tickets
Theater tickets
Railroad tickets
Drawing instruction books
Wallpaper
*Catalogues
Old stencils
Decalcomania sheets
Tea-paper napkins—earliest paper napkins
Party favor bonbons—the kind that snapped. Older than you
    think

53. *Pewter*

English
American
Chinese
*Britannia ware—a development of pewter, often mistaken for it.
    Britannia was spun, not molded. Flourished in America from
    1810 on
Porringers
Tankards
Chargers—serving platters
Basins
Plates
Flagons—vessels for wine with handles, spout, and lid
Platters
Candlesticks
Inkwells
Measures
Teapots—commonest in britannia
Coffee urns

Cuspidors
Shaving mugs
Snuffboxes
Lamps
Apothecary measures
Spoons

54. *Personalized Items*

Today we go in heavily for personalized items of all kinds. The idea is not new. There were many things marked with the names or initials of individuals in the years in which our antiques have originated. Names may be well known or obscure.

Shaving mugs
Mustache cups
Souvenir mugs
Children's mugs
Tonic bottles
Souvenir glass from resorts
Silver pieces
Samplers
Signed pictures

55. *Political Items*

Posters
Torches
Banners
Flags
Canes
*Buttons—campaign
Ribbons
Badges
Plates
Handkerchiefs
Mugs
Campaign post cards
Glass portrait bottles
Currier and Ives prints

*Lincolniana
Flasks
Slogan bottles

56. *Professions*

Aside from the commercial concerns who have gathered together the antiques relating to their various businesses there are many individuals who like to collect the things from the early days of their own professions or businesses. Suggested here are a few:

Dressmaker
  Fashion books, prints, and magazines
  Fashion dolls
  Patterns
  Materials
  Sewing equipment— (see No. 48)
Barber
  Shaving mugs
  Tonic bottles
  Barber plates—made with cutout in rim for holding close
    under the chin when shaving
  Brush holders
  Shaving paper vases
  Soap cups
  Razors
Pretzel manufacturer
  Pretzel bottles—in shape of pretzel
  Toast racks—with series of pretzel as dividers
  Prints
  Signs
Conjurer
  Old sleight-of-hand material
  Magic trick equipment
  Posters and handbills of old magic shows
Dairyman
  Milk bottles

Cans
Pans
Skimmers
Old cream separators
Cheese-making utensils
Butter molds
Churns
Milk pails
Ice-cream molds
Chemist
Glassware
Laboratory equipment
Photographer
Cameras
Darkroom equipment
Old photograph albums
Daguerreotypes
Tintypes
Street-photographer's portraits
Post-card portraits
Decorator
Wallpaper
Drapery and upholstery materials
Old style books for furniture, etc.
Catalogues
Medical doctor
Medicine bottles and cases
Old prescription books
Surgical instruments
Tongue depressors
Quassia cups—made of quassia wood which imparted a bitter
    taste to water kept in it
Cupping glasses—small glass cups used as suction cups for
    relieving congestion made by burning a paper spill in
    them to create a vacuum
Bleeding cups
Bedpans—even Bennington made these. Some in pewter

Druggist
   Apothecary jars
   Ointment or salve pots
   Drug bottles
   Window-display bottles for colored water
   Leech jars—in which the bloodsuckers were kept on the
      counter
   Sponge baskets—wire
   Candy jars
   Pill slabs for rolling pills
   Old prescription files
   Scales
   Mortars and pestles
   Shop signs
Optician— (see No. 49)
Grocer— (see No. 60)
Railroad man
   Toy trains
   Train models
   Timetables
   Lanterns
   Watches
   Caps
   Emblems of various roads

57. *Religious Items*

Jewish
   *All the fine Jewish ceremonial pieces, torahs and torah
      finials, menorahs, spice and citron boxes, silver, brass,
      and ceramic pieces
Protestant
   Early silver and pewter church pieces, baptismal basins,
      salvers, beakers, communion cups
   *Bibles
   Collection plates and baskets
   Sunday-school cards
   Prayer books

Hymnals
Primitive Bible prints
Religious pictures
Old pews
Church lighting fixtures
Bells
Catholic
Candlesticks—altar
Statues—silver, wood, ceramic, plaster, stone
Medals
Altar bells
*Rosaries and rosary cases
Crucifixes
Holy-water fonts
Holy pictures
Primitive Spanish *santos* or *bultos*—religious pictures and
figures
Missals—books containing liturgy of church services
Prayer books
Illuminated pages from old church books
Stations of the Cross
Vigil lamps

58. *Scrimshaw Bone and Ivory*

*Scrimshaw was the name given to etching pictures on bone,
teeth, and tusks of whale and walrus. Sailors made it into many
useful and ornamental pieces on their long voyages

Busk boards
Powder horns
Pie crimpers or jagging wheels
Rolling pins
Butter knives
Napkin rings
Clothespins
Spoons
Jackstraws
Chessmen

Dominoes
Cribbage boards
Back scratchers
Cane heads
Snuffboxes
Knitting needles
Workbaskets
Bodkins
Necklaces
Bracelets
Watch holders
Toys
Vases
Showpieces—decorated tusks

59. *Sports*

All the sports of today had a beginning, some quite far back in history. It is the earlier paraphernalia that the collector will be interested in and will probably recognize quicker than the dealer in antiques. Thus he may find:

Golf items—trophies, motifs on steins, matchsafes, etc., balls, clubs, bags, and old golfing costumes for both men and women
Tennis—old rule books, motifs on jewelry, etc., old rackets, etc.
Winter sports—skates, sleds, skis, snowshoes, curling stones
Croquet—sets, prints, etc.
Boxing—gloves, prints, posters
Fishing tackle
Bows and arrows
Traps and snares
*Decoys—carved ducks and other birds used as lures by hunters
Target balls
Trapshooting "pigeons"
Shooting-gallery birds

60. *Store Items*

There has been a tremendous zoom in interest in items from old stores, particularly the general country store. Private collectors have turned their collections into museums which, because of nostalgia, attract the transient visitor. This is a good field for the beginner to investigate because items are still available and not too expensive. They include:

Old containers
Bins of wood and tin for keeping tea, coffee, flour, grains, cereals, spices, etc. Many of these are quite handsome, with colored transfer pictures, gold labels, mirrors, drawers, etc.
*Canisters—small versions of the bins with lift lids
Jars—especially candy jars
Cooky tins and cracker tins
Scoops
Scales
Coffee grinders
Brooms
Old calicoes
Sunbonnets
Pot-bellied stoves
Spittoons
Spool cabinets
Lamps

*61. Tea Caddies

Tea caddies (from the Chinese word katty, a measure) make very interesting collections, as they can be found in so many wares, early and late. These were chests for the precious tea, often supplied with lock and key. They usually contained two glass or pewter jars for two kinds of tea.

China
Silver
Pewter—including Chinese pewter
Wood—made in many period styles, such as Sheraton, etc.
Tortoise shell
Papier-mâché
Wooden fruit forms—apples, pears, etc., of fruit woods
Tin—including English Pontypool

Brass
Copper

62. *Tobacco*

*Tobacco jars
Pouches
Tobacco cutters
    Advertising items
    Novelty shapes
Cigar cases—hand painted, leather, decalcomania decorations
Cigar clippers
Cigar lighters
Cigar bands
Humidors
*Pipes
    Meerschaum
    Porcelain
    Clay
    Novelty
Pipe tampers
Pipe tongs
Dutch and German brass tobacco boxes
Britannia boxes
*Tin tobacco boxes
Labeled matchboxes
Pocket matchboxes
Old matches—pack—wax
Cigar-store signs
Cigar-store Indians and other figures
*Cigarette cards

63. *Tools*

*Tools of the trades
    Carpenter
    Cabinetmaker
    Mason
    Glazier
    Turner

Watchmaker
Combmaker
Cooper
Ship's carpenter
Silversmith
Pewterer
Blacksmith
Jeweler
Brazier
Surveyor
Architect
Toolboxes
Conestoga-wagon boxes
Grindstones
Jacks

64. *Toys*

*Pull toys
    Tin
    Iron
Mechanical
    Wind-up
    Friction
    Steam
Transportation toys
    Trains
    Trolleys
    Wagons
    Carriages
    Boats
*Train sets
Bell toys
Squeak toys
*Cap pistols
Paper-cap exploders
*Schoenhut Circus toys
Marbles

Tops
Puzzles
*Whistles
Horns
Drums
Jumping jacks
Jack-in-the-boxes
Monkey-on-the-sticks
Kites
Toys made to move by heat or sand wheels
Folded cutouts
Wooden toys
    Noah's arks
    Toy kitchens
    Toy stores
    Wagons
    Hobbyhorses
Pop-up books
Rattles
Stuffed animals
Teething rings

65. *Trivets*

*Trivets—stands for pots or dishes at the fireplace or stands for pressing irons are a big collectible. The early ones are wrought iron and more desirable.

Wrought Iron
    Heart shape
    Tulip
    Spade
    Circular
    Oval
    Square
    Triangular
    Horseshoe
    Geometric patterns
    Gridiron

Star
With wooden handles
Cast-iron trivets and iron stands
 Many of the above designs
 Garfield
 Love birds
 Cherubs
 Order of Cincinnati
 Odd Fellows
 G.A.R.
 Lincoln Drape
 Fireman
 Serpent
 Washington
 Eagle and heart
 Mottoes—good luck, etc.
 Trade phrases
 Initials of the makers
Brass
 Footmen—four-legged stands for hot-water kettle or hot plates
 English three-footed iron-legged trivets with brass plate tops
  patterned in
   Animal figures,
   Conventional designs,
   Floral designs,
   Compass.
 Chippendale fretwork
 Fire-bar trivets with brass perforated tops and two hooks to
  hang on fireguard as warmers
 Small brass trivets
 Cast-brass table trivets

66. *Personages*

Many famous persons in history appear again and again in all kinds of wares. If you have an admiration for or curiosity about some particular figure, you might make this the basis for your collection.

General Washington
Lafayette
Ben Franklin
Lincoln
Shakespeare
Queen Victoria
Napoleon
Jenny Lind
Dickens
Beethoven
Schiller
General Kosciusko
Tyler
Harrison
Garfield
McKinley

67. *Valentines*

*This is such a large and popular area of collecting that it deserves a special heading.

Early homemade—painted and with fancy papers
Pinpricked
Scissors cutwork
Rebus
Puzzle
Lace and embossed—Howland, Whitney, etc. 1850 on
Embroidered
Hairwork
Woven
Lithographed
Quilted
Celluloid
Painted on silk or satin
Comic
Valentine objects other than cards
Three-dimensional

Valentine kits
Old "writers," books of Valentine verse

68. *Warmers*

Foot warmers—square boxes with perforated tin sides for holding
hot coals
Hand and muff warmers
Bed warmers—(see No. 13)
Night warmers—for baby's milk or for invalid use with open com-
partment for small lamp or candle underneath. Called *veil-
leuses,* or night watchmen. Made in tin and ceramics
Soapstone—this stone held heat for carriage or bed
Hot-water bottles of stoneware
Plate warmers—tin cabinets with shelves and back open to the
fire. An early fireplace item
Hot-water dish warmers—double dish with hot water in the bot-
tom. Found in old china as well as metal
Samovars
Tea urns
Brass teakettle with spirit lamp—Victorian item.

69. *Weather Items*

Weather vanes
Thermometers
Barometers—a good field. From the fine English pieces to the
novelties
*Almanacs

70. *Woodenware or Treen*

Tunbridge—named for the English town where this fine mosaic
or parquetry ware was made
Burl—wood cut from a knot or malformation on a tree trunk.
Gives interesting graining and considered very fine for bowls,
etc.
Lehnware—small painted wooden pieces made by a Pennsylvania
Dutchman near Lancaster. Spice boxes, sugar buckets, trinket
boxes much sought for. A more or less souvenir or "gift"
item of the late 1800's

Carved pieces—mostly Pennsylvania Dutch—eagles, toys, mantel ornaments, Noah's ark, and putz animals, etc.

Shaker boxes—kitchen boxes of fine workmanship made by the members of the Shaker sect from maple with pine hoops and copper brads

Bellows—many in plain wood, others painted

Souvenir transfer-printed pieces

*Household articles

    Bowls

    Plates

    Spoons

    Ladles

    Boxes

    Cutting boards and pastry boards

    Churns

    Dough boxes

    Cranberry rakes

    Ox yokes

    Knife boxes

    Gun racks

    Yarn winders—*Niddy-noddies,* as they were called

    Shoe lasts

    Grain measures

    Grain sifters—with hair mesh, called a *temse*

    Sugar tubs

    Maple syrup buckets

    Featherbed beaters—long, flat instruments for fluffing up the feathers

    Mantle presser—a clothes presser, long, heavy board, with handle, often primitively carved

    Accordion folding hatrack—with white china knobs to hang on the wall

    Newspaper racks—wall pieces with hinged pockets for papers

    Venetian blinds cornices—many early ones were carved or fretwork wood

    Spinning wheels

    Looms

71. *Miscellaneous*

*Miniaturia—the tiny things, including dollhouse items

*Kate Greenaway items—reflecting the popularity of this illustrator of children's books in the late 1800's. Greenaway figures found in ceramics, buttons, cards, etc.

Sunbonnet babies—an early 1900 popular subject

*Bookmarks—very rewarding collectible for beginners

Stevengraphs—pictures woven into silk ribbons—used often for bookmarks. Named for maker

Identification stamps and brands for

    Cattle

    Logging irons

    Grain sacks

    Barrels

    Furniture

    Silver

    Brass

    Pewter

Gavels

*Daguerreotype cases

Photo albums

Straw marquetry—straw inlay work

Phrenology items—pieces reflecting the fad for "reading" the shape of the head, charts, inkwells with marked heads, etc.

Globes

    Terrestial

    Celestial

Exercisers and health-apparatus pieces—such as dumbbells and Indian clubs

Miniature books—many can be found measuring not over two inches

Dried bouquets and funeral wreaths—Victorian pieces under glass

Left-handed items

Three-handled items

Fret-sawed work—shelves, etc.

Handcuffs and shackles

*Baskets—other than straw. Interesting basket shapes in china, glass, and silver, including brides' baskets

Toothpicks—gold, ivory, scrimshaw

Pearl-handled tableware

Tiebacks—for curtains

    Brass—(see No. 9)

    Wood

    Iron

    Glass—particularly Sandwich rosettes

    Mercury glass

Mirror knobs and wall pegs

Fancy nails for picture hanging

Doorknobs

    Sandwich glass

    Cut glass

    Bennington pottery

    China—Dresden

    Iron

Traveling items

Photo frames

Lavabos—a washstand on the wall consisting of a water cistern with faucet and bowl attached or separate. Range is from 1390 to 1890

    Silver

    Iron

    Tole—tin over iron

    Painted tin

    Glass

    Majolica

    Redware

    Stoneware

    Pewter

    Sheffield

    Ironstone

    Wood

What's-Its—mysterious things without identity.